FERRARI DINO 246 GT

Nathan Beehl

CONTENTS

Foulis

Haynes

ISBN 0 85429 576 3

A FOULIS Motoring Book

First published 1987

© **Haynes Publishing Group**

Published by:
Haynes Publishing Group,
Sparkford, Near Yeovil,
Somerset BA22 7JJ

Haynes Publications Inc.
861 Lawrence Drive, Newbury
Park, California 91320, USA

**British Library Cataloguing in
Publication Data**
Beehl, Nathan
    Ferrari Dino super profile.—(Super
    profile)
    1. Dino automobile—History
    I. Title II. Series
    629.2'222   TL215.D5
ISBN 0-85429-576-3

Library of Congress catalog card number
86-82629

Editor: Mansur Darlington
Dust jacket design: Rowland
Smith
Series photographer: Andrew
Morland
Road tests: Courtesy of *Motor* and
Road and Track
Page layout: Peter Kay
Printed in England, by:
J.H. Haynes & Co. Ltd

Further titles in this series will be published at regular
intervals. For information on new titles please contact
your bookseller or write to the publisher.

FOREWORD

The Dino and I were just getting to know one another. Together we were making fast but relaxed progress down a meandering minor road, when we came behind a trio of slower cars that impeded our progress. "That's the problem with these roads," said my passenger, "there's too much traffic." I snicked the gear lever into second and, on a short straight, pressed down on the accelerator. "Yes, but it's the best reason there is for having a Dino," said I, as we sailed past.

For me, the beauty of the Ferrari Dino is that in a very short while it instils confidence in its driver. Admittedly it doesn't have the push-in-the-back urge of the Boxer or the Daytona (the subject of a previous Super Profile) – and possibly for that reason doesn't have the same intimidating effect – but the way it performs and handles relaxes one immediately. It may only have half the cylinders of the traditional Ferrari, but it's more than half the car. When Ferrari launched the car the sales brochure said, 'Tiny, brilliant, safe ... almost a Ferrari'. Most owners today will tell you that the Dino has lived down the 'almost' tag, and is now, as it deserves to be, a

part of Ferrari history. I would like to thank the following for helping me relate the Dino story, and for their time and assistance. First, my thanks to Rod Grainger for the opportunity to write this book, and to Andrew Morland who took the bulk of the photos. Keith Bluemel and John Gould both lent photos from their own collections, and Pininfarina supplied photos of the various prototypes and styling exercises. Graypaul Motors and Dino Services helped with technical information. Terry Murphy provided the red coupé, Miles Wilkins the blue coupé, and Alan Tucknott the red spyder that features in the bulk of the photos.

Terry Murphy and Jeff Simpson bravely submitted to the spotlight in the face and switched on tape recorder for the 'Owner's View' section. Denny Schue has done sterling work with his Dino Register and was very helpful with chassis numbers and chronological information. Finally a word of thanks to my long suffering wife, Rosalind Jane, who not only patched up my two blistered typing fingers, but also put up with having her holiday interrupted so that I could finish this manuscript.

Nathan Beehl

HISTORY

The First Dino engine

Alfredo (Dino) Ferrari was the only son of Enzo and Laura Ferrari. Enzo met Laura in Turin, as he recalled in his biography *'My Terrible Joys'*. ''I married very young, somewhere around 1920; I cannot remember the exact date as I have mislaid the marriage certificate. I had arrived in Turin only a short time before, with an old trunk and some rather rough and ready manners. One evening under the arcades of Porta Nuova, I happened to make the acquaintance of a pretty and smartly dressed little blonde with a vivacious manner. I was smitten and, although I did not know it then, she was shortly afterwards to become my wife. Her parents, a hard-working couple in modest circumstances who hailed from the

village of Racconigi some twenty miles away, were at first against our marrying, but they eventually decided to give us their blessings and the Turinese girl thus set up house with the young man from Modena. The latter's means were limited; indeed, they consisted of nothing but ambitions and hopes; but as we know, young men and old men are alike given to aphorisms, and this young man declared, in fact, that nothing else mattered where there was love. I later came to realize that the rest did matter, and mattered a lot.''

In January 1932 Alfredo (named after Ferrari's sadly deceased older brother) was born. Being Ferrari's only son it was natural that he should be groomed to take his place in his father's business, and so his eduction was engineering oriented. He studied for his diploma at the Corli Technical Institute in Modena, and then moved to Switzerland to take a degree. He chose as his thesis a project for a 1.5-litre, 4-cylinder engine with three valves per cylinder, two intake and one exhaust. He also studied economy and commerce at the University of Bologna, and naturally worked at the factory. Dino's first car was a little Fiat Topolino; this was followed by another Fiat, this time a 1100TV, and he also had the use of a Ferrari 2-litre in which he used to enjoy himself on the Modena test track. It is believed that this car was rebodied by Scaglietti from a design supplied by Dino, and which was subsequently copied for the first 750 Monza. Sadly, the young man suffered from ill health, and on 30 June 1956, at the age of 24 he died. In his autobiography, Enzo Ferrari says that his son died from a Nephris virus, which was a result of Dino's muscular dystrophy. This disease has also been stated as causing the death of Laura Ferrari who died on 27 February 1978. What is certain, though, is that Dino spent his last few months confined to bed for

long periods. Enzo Ferrari credits his son with ideal of using a V6 layout for the small capacity engine that Ferrari needed for the 1957 Formula 2 season. ''I and my old friend Jano [engineer and designer Vittorio Jano] spent long hours at his bedside, discussing with him the design of a $1\frac{1}{2}$-litre engine. This could be either a 4-cylinder, a straight 6, a 65 degree V6 or an 8-cylinder. I remember how carefully and with what competence Dino read and discussed all the notes and reports that were brought to him daily from Maranello. For reasons of mechanical efficiency, he finally came to the conclusion that the engine should be a V6, and we accepted this decision. There was thus born the famous 156, (1.5-litre, 6-cylinder) which was to burst into song for the first time in November 1956, five months after Dino had passed away.'' In honour of his lost son this V6 engine was called Dino.

Interestingly, Jano had already had experience of V6s having produced the outstanding Aurelia V6 for Lancia. The engine he designed for Ferrari had twin overhead camshafts per bank, and two spark plugs per cylinder supplied by twin magnetos. Fuel was fed in via three twin-choke Weber 38DCNs. According to the Ferrari publication *'Caratteristiche tecniche dei motori Ferrari realizzati dal 1946 al 1985'*, this little package produced 180bhp; the contemporary British F2 engine, the Coventry Climax, was quoted as producing 140bhp. In its first Formula 2 race, at Reims, Luigi Musso used the V6's power advantage to take the winner's laurels. The Dino engine had arrived.

Meanwhile the sport's governing body had announced a change in the regulations for Grand Prix cars for the 1958 season, and Enzo Ferrari was already looking at using the Dino. The $2\frac{1}{2}$-litre maximum capacity regulation was retained, but the use of alcohol-based fuels was banned, only straight petrol, albeit up to 130 octane, could be used. As the Formula 2 Dino 156 engine had been designed to run on petrol, and as it had already shown some very encouraging power outputs, the decision was taken to develop it for the 1958 Grand Prix car. After a number of interim enlargements Ferrari finished up with an engine of 2417cc, and thus was born the Dino 246 engine (well, the first 246, anyway, as we shall see later). History relates how the 246 engine carried Mike Hawthorn to victory in the World Drivers Championship, the first Englishman to win this coveted title, although the moral champion was undoubtedly Stirling Moss who scored four victories to Hawthorn's one.

But revolution was on its way, and in 1959 the rear engined Cooper-Climax brought Jack Brabham his first World Championship. Brabham and Cooper repeated this feat in 1960, although the last victory for a front-engined car in World Championship Grand Prix racing went to Phil Hill, the American driver, in a Ferrari Dino 246. By 1961 the revolution was complete. The regulations for Grand Prix cars were changed and the capacity limit was now 1.5 litres. The rear-engined Coopers and Lotuses had shown that the front-engined car had had its day, and the line-up for the first race of 1961 looked very different from the last one of 1960.

At the 1966 Paris Salon Pininfarina showed another styling exercise, which although not based on the 206 looked very much like one, at least from the outside. Inside it was certainly different as there were three seats, with the driver sat in the centre and slightly forward of his passengers. The outline was similar to that of the Dino 206GT Speciale shown the previous year, but at the front instead of the full width perspex headlight cover there was a wide oval grille flanked by a single headlight each side, each one having its own streamlined clear perspex cover. Beneath each headlight was a small curved chromed bumper reaching back almost as far as the front wheel arch. The front of this car, the 365P, was almost pure 206/246GT, so although not a Dino there were definitely strong styling elements that would be repeated on the Dino road car.

The Turin Motor Show just a few weeks later was a major event as far as the Dino chronology was concerned. Here a second prototype, 'Dino Berlinetta GT' was shown, and also a Fiat Dino Spider 2000, so the journalists had plenty to go at with these two. The Dino was almost there as far as the 206GT was concerned. Overall there would be few changes between this version and the final production car, the main change being that the engine cover, which on this car was still one piece, being hinged from the trailing edge of the roof and stretching right to the rear tail panel, would be redesigned for easier handling. The wheels, which were five-spoke alloy in the style of the Ferrari sports-prototypes of the period, would also be changed.

Fiat's Dino-engined sports car turned out to be in the traditional front-engined, rear wheel drive configuration with a swoopy body-line and a cut-off Kamm tail. The front featured four headlights, in pairs, with wide indicators set outside of these. This design detail was reminiscent of the 1965 Paris Show Dino but without the perspex cover. The engine was a 2-litre version of the V6 Dino, and the production of this car would see the necessary units manufactured to assure Ferrari its use in Formula 2 racing in 1967.

Meanwhile, back on the circuits Ferrari had produced a delightful little car for the up to 2-litre class in sports car racing.

Ferrari had intended to produce enough (50) of the 206S to qualify it as a Group 4 (ie production) car, but due to industrial problems managed to make less than twenty. The engine was the 2-litre version of the Dino V6 with single-plug ignition, a revised combustion chamber, and a lower compression ratio. Fuel was fed through Weber 40DCN2s, although Lucas fuel injection was tried on some cars. Ferrari quoted the power output as 205bhp @ 8800rpm. The bodywork was by Drogo, and looked like a down-sized version of the 4-litre prototype 330P3. The 206S is undoubtedly one of the best looking sports-racing cars ever made, and well illustrates the Italian flair for style. For example the wings don't just cover the wheels, they also have to look sharp, so each wing has a small crease running the length of the curvature. It serves no useful purpose, it's hardly noticeable, yet it's there! The 206S also achieved some notable results including second on the Targa Florio when driven by Baghetti/Guichet and second also in the Nürburgring 1000km with Bandini/Scarfiotti sharing the driving.

The Second Dino Engine

But where did this leave Ferrari? It left him where he always is when there's a new set of regulations – ready and waiting. It also introduced the second type of V6 Dino engine. This was the 120 degree engine developed by engineer Carlo Chiti, who was also responsible for the distinctive twin-opening 'nostril nose' or 'shark nose' look. The wider angle of the 120 degree Vee allowed for better top engine design and so this became the number one unit with the 65 degree engine being used as a back-up. Due to the superiority of the Dino engine over the opposition Ferrari scored five victories in eight races with three drivers, Von Trips winning in Holland and England, Phil Hill in Belgium and Italy, and newcomer Baghetti in France. Ferrari won the Constructors Championship and Phil Hill became the first American to win the World Drivers Championship.

IN 1962 and 1963 the Ferrari was outpaced by the better handling BRM and Lotus designs and – dare we say it? – by their more powerful engines. Ferrari's only victory in two years was that scored by John Surtees in the 1963 German Grand Prix at the famous Nürburgring.

For the two remaining years of the 1½-litre formula Ferrari employed an 8-cylinder and even a 12-cylinder engine. The 8-cylinder engine powered John Surtees to the Drivers World Championship in 1964, but as far as 6-cylinder Grand Prix Ferraris are concerned that was it until the advent of the 1½-litre turbo engined car of 1981, and that engine is beyond the scope of our narrative. Our engine first appeared in 1965.

In March 1965 it was announced that there was to be collaboration between Ferrari and Fiat, because Fiat were looking for an engine for a projected high-performance road car. The co-operation between the two companies would also benefit Ferrari because the engine would qualify to be the basis for the 1967 Formula 2 car. The motor sport's governing body had decreed that as from 1967 the regulations for Formula 2 would raise the maximum capacity allowed from 1000cc to 1600cc, but, here's the rub, the engine had to be based on a production unit with a minimum of 500 cars made per year. In view of the fact that Ferrari's production in 1964, the year before the announcement, was only 654 cars in total there was no way that Ferrari would be able to build 500 of one type of

car in order to qualify for the new Formula 2; but with Fiat's help that obstacle was overcome.

The first appearance of the Rocchi-developed Dino engine was in April 1965 when Ferrari entered the pretty little Dino 166P in the Monza 1000km sports car race. The engine was an advanced version of Jano's original design with a 77mm bore and 57mm stroke, giving a capacity of 1592cc. It still had the 65 degree angle between the cylinders and two overhead camshafts per bank. With twin ignition and three twin-choke Weber 40DCOs the new engine was rated at 175bhp @ 9000rpm. The car itself was a two-seater coupé sports car, with a low waist-line which had the effect of making the windscreen and roof look very tall; yet in reality the car was lower than the famed Ford GT40, being only 39 inches high. The chassis and suspension design followed the contemporary Grand Prix car practice, and some even described it as a two-seat Formula 1 car. The little red coupé proved to be very quick, and at the Nürburgring 1000km finished fourth overall, ahead of two Cobra-Daytonas and the Shelby Ford GT40. Such was its performance that some doubted that it was only 1600cc, but a post race scrutineering session verified it as such. The little coupé also ran at Le Mans but retired after the engine blew up. The coupé was then entered in the European Mountain Climb Championship and made its début on 11 July at the Trento-Bondone event in Italy. For this event Ferrari fitted an enlarged Dino engine with a displacement of 1987cc. This was achieved by boring out the 166 engine to 86mm, and the quoted power output was 205bhp @ 8800rpm. Scarfiotti, who had won the Mountain Climb Championship in 1962, was entrusted with the driving chores, and won this event and three others to become the 1965 Champion.

Meanwhile at Fiat, Ferrari and Pininfarina developments were continuing on the various awaited road cars, and proof of this was seen at the Paris Salon in October 1965.

First Dino Car

The car on display was called 'Dino 206GT Speciale', and was based on a racing car chassis with the mid-mounted V6 situated in-line. Of particular interest was the body that clothed this new prototype, because there were a number of features that would eventually appear on the production version of the Dino. The complete car was very low, looking hardly big enough for an average size person. The profile was almost pure Dino except for the nose which was slightly lengthened where a full width, faired-in plexiglass moulding covered double paired headlamps, above which a yellow Dino nose badge was affixed. The nose was low with pronounced humps over the front wheels and a steadily raising waist line which fell away over the rear wheels. Below the side window there was a long scooped duct that fed air to the engine compartment. This had a thin chrome high-light strip running from front to back that also incorporated the door-pull. The rear window echoed a 1954 design on a 375 chassis that Pininfarina built for Ingrid Bergman, being vertical with the ends folded round like an extremely wide letter U. This feature was repeated on the production 206GT and 246GTs. Another feature that found its way onto the production cars was the unobtrusive yet effective crease line running along the body at mid-wheel height. The overall effect was quite striking, and indicated the direction Pininfarina was taking.

Birth of the 206GT

And so the appearance of the Dino 246GT moved nearer. In 1967 another step along the way was taken with the début of the latest prototype model of the 206GT. This made its bow at the Turin show in November, and now had the V6 turned through 90 degrees, and mounted across the chassis behind the passenger compartment. Yes, this definitely looked like a practical road car. (Practical being used here, of course, in the Ferrari sense of the word.) Mounting the engine sideways meant that there was at least some space that looked as if some luggage could be squeezed into it, as long as the cases weren't too big. The front under-bonnet area was filled by the spare wheel. The engine was the same as that used for the fiat Dino but with a new sump, cast by Ferrari, which enclosed the gearbox and differential in a one-piece casing. Although the gearbox was mated to the engine the design was such that the lubrication system for the transmission was separate from that of the engine. Ferrari naturally tinkered with the engine and claimed that the reworked air intakes and a special exhaust system, amongst other things, added 20bhp over the standard Fiat unit. The wheels were those from the Fiat Dino and had racing style three-ear knock-off hubcaps fitted. The body was now definitive Dino with three opening panels, one at the front for the spare wheel, and two at the rear, one over the engine, and, behind that, one over the luggage area. The chassis followed racing practice of the time with independent suspension all round, servo-assisted disc brakes, and rack and pinion steering. With such a package it is no wonder that the journalists of the time couldn't wait to try one, but even

Paul Frère (who won Le Mans in 1960 at the wheel of a Ferrari) could only give his impression from the passenger seat. Still, his chauffeur was a certain Enzo Ferrari. Frère's feeling was that ''it corners as flat as a kipper, seems to be perfectly neutral and is incredibly agile''. It seems he liked it.

The same year at the Frankfurt show, Pininfarina presented a styling exercise with a Dino badge on the nose. Called the 'Dino Berlinetta Prototipo Competizione' it had a family resemblance to the 206GT, but they definitely were not twins. This one had a circular roof line when viewed from the front, and gull wing doors. The roof proper was no more than a couple of inches wide, the doors being hinged from this. The side windows came right up to the centre-line hinge and down to the waist line, making almost the total roof area a large glass dome. Quite how the glass roof was compatible with the needs of a competition car wasn't explained, but the competition aspect was emphasised by the large adjustable flat-plane aerodynamic wings mounted fore and aft of the bodywork. It was certainly an unusual design and not generally regarded as one of Pininfarina's better efforts.

The next appearance of the 206GT was at the Brussels Salon 1968, and apart from a few minor finishing details this was almost the production car. When production began in spring 1969 it was noticed that quarter-lights had been added to the side windows, and the perspex headlight covers had been removed. And so at last the 'almost a Ferrari' Ferrari had appeared. The production versions had the bodies built in aluminium by Scaglietti, and had the Fiat Dino-style wheels fitted by means of centre-lock knock-off spinners. The Dino was well reported on, with the handling and roadholding especially being mentioned as

outstanding. Naturally the performance also impressed, with a 0-60mph time of less than 7 seconds and a top speed of more than 140mph. And all from only 2 litres.

It was soon decided that the Dino could handle more power, and indeed needed it if it was going to keep ahead of the Porsche 911 which was perceived, at least by journalists, as being the Dino's main competitor. And so, at the Geneva Salon in March 1969 a new Dino prototype, the 246GT, was displayed.

The 246GT

At first glance there seems no difference between the two Dinos, but put them side by side and one soon notices the longer wheelbase of the 246, and also the neat little cover for the fuel filler cap. But what one couldn't see was that the body was now made of steel, instead of aluminium, and the engine block was iron, and not alloy. These changes made the 246GT more than 300lb heavier than its predecessor, but the enlarged engine produced an extra 15bhp to cope with the additional weight. The new engine had the displacement increased to 2418cc. This was achieved by enlarging the bore and stroke to 92.5 x 60.0mm, and this in turn increased the power output to 195bhp @ 7600rpm, and the torque to 166lbf ft @ 5500rpm. In real terms this knocked a few tenths of a second off the 0-60mph time and added about 8mph to the top speed.

November 1969 saw the 246GT officially launched as a production car, at the Turin Show. What had started out as a styling exercise on a racing car chassis at the Paris Salon in October 1965 was now a fully developed racing car for the road. The chassis followed usual Ferrari practice, being constructed from oval-section tubes braced by rectangular-section cross tubing. A large section oval tube ran down the centre of the chassis from front to rear through which the water pipes to the radiator were run. Underneath the chassis was a glass-fibre panel to give some measure of weather protection, and above the chassis was fitted a glass-fibre tub, and some smaller moulded pieces that formed the passenger compartment, front and rear bulkheads, spare wheel housing etc. Fore and aft of this main chassis were narrower sub-assemblies for mounting the suspension components and for supporting the radiators at the front and the engine assembly at the rear. Front suspension was by means of pressed steel unequal length wishbones attached to the chassis by four adjustable eye bolts, with co-axial springs and Koni shock absorbers looking after the necessary movements. A 16mm roll bar was positioned by rubber bushes, and affixed to the lower wishbone by forged links. Rear suspension was basically the same as at the front, except that the coil/damper was mounted above the top wishbone. Brakes were Girling discs on all four corners with a servo-assisted dual system to lessen pedal pressure. Knock-on Cromodora 14 x 6^1/$_2$ inch wheels with 185VR14 tyres were fitted as standard. As has already been established the engine was a 65 degree V6 with a bore and stroke of 92.5 x 60.0mm, a cast iron block and alloy cylinder heads, with two chain driven overhead camshafts per bank of cylinders. The fuel feed was by means of three twin-choke Weber 40DCNF/7 carburettors. A Marelli distributor with coil provided the necessary electrical impulses to spin the unit round to a 7600rpm redline. Because the engine was mounted sideways in the chassis the gearbox was alongside and parallel to the crankshaft. This necessitated the fitting of a set of

three helical spur gears to transfer the power down to the gearbox. Five forward gears with Porsche syncromesh, and a reverse gear were housed in three castings which allowed the engine and transmission oils to be kept separated. Solid drive shafts with constant velocity joints at both ends connected the drive to the rear wheels.

Inside, the Dino was a genuine two-seater with no pretensions of being anything other than an out-and-out sports car. It was surprising though that the seats didn't have adjustable backrests, although the seat could be pushed back far enough to allow adequate legroom for all except a Harlem Globetrotter. In front of the driver was an aluminium-spoked, leather-rimmed steering wheel with the Dino script replacing the more usual prancing horse in the steering wheel boss. Through the steering wheel the eight main instruments could be seen, housed in an elliptical facia like that of its contemporary and stable mate, the Ferrari Daytona. In the centre of the dash were four small instruments for the oil temperature, water temperature, oil pressure and fuel capacity. The Veglia electronic tachometer was on the left, and an optimistic 270kmh speedometer on the right. To the far left was another small instrument, the ammeter, and right over in the other corner was the clock. This, then, was the first series (type L) Dino 246GT.

In 1970 the so-called second series (type M) Dino was produced. It should be said here, however, that the Dino, by virtue of being a hand-built auto, was subject to continual change, and some second series modifications have been found on first series cars. Major changes included swapping from Girling to ATE brakes, and changing from knock-on to bolt-on hubs, although the wheel pattern stayed the same. On the chassis only the

suspension lower mounts were now adjustable. The engine had different Dinoplex ignition, and a changed exhaust system, and inside, a Momo steering wheel was fitted. 1970 was also a landmark year as far as the British market was concerned because the first right-hand drive Dino made its appearance.

The third Series (type E) appeared a year later, in 1971. This can be distinguished by the single fuel pump (earlier cars had two) and a modified gearbox. A six-lobe distributor cam was now standard, and on the outside, the number plate light was moved to the boot lid, instead of being hidden inside the ends of the rear bumperettes.

It was also in 1971 that the US version made its début. Due to the United States safety and anti-smog regulations, the Americans had to make do with a heavier and less powerful Dino than the Europeans. In order to meet the anti-smog Federal emission limits Ferrari fitted an air injection pump to dilute the exhaust gases. This automatically cutout at 3500rpm in order to maintain power on the top-end, but even so the US Dino loses some 20bhp to its less restricted brothers. The additional anti-smog fittings, and other mandatory equipment such as turn signals in the front and rear wings, increased the weight by about 50lb for the US version, and naturally had an adverse effect on performance. *Road and Track* magazine recorded a 0-60mph time of nearly eight seconds; considered slow for a car of this type.

The 246GTS Dino Spyder

The Dino reached its production peak in 1972 with the arrival of the GTS version, the letter 'S' standing for spyder, which in reality translates into a car with a removable roof. The roof section lifts out and can be stowed behind the seats resulting in what is commonly called a 'Targa' top. The GTS was particularly popular in the American market, but right-hand drive cars were also available in spyder form and these are particularly sought after today.

An interesting 'option package' also became available in 1972. It seems that no specific name was given to the package by the factory, but enthusiasts generally refer to it as the 'Daytona package', because part of the option included seats of the same style as those found in the Ferrari Daytona. The second part of the package featured $7^1/2$ x 14 inch Campagnolo wheels to replace the narrower Cromodoras that were standard fitting. The wheel arches had extended flares to cover the wider rubber. The purpose of producing the 'Daytona package' may have been in order to qualify the 246GT as a competitive Group 4 racing car, Group 4 being at that time a class for production based cars, which included, amongst others, the Ferrari Daytona and the Porsche 911. This may also be linked with the appearance of a 246GT in the classic Le Mans 24 Hours in the same year. Although prepared by the factory, this car was entered by Luigi Chinetti's North American Racing Team, more commonly known by the initials only, hence NART. Chinetti had been a long-time friend and collaborator with Ferrari, having given the Ferrari marque their first win in the French classic back in 1949, and on many occassions had been entrusted with the competition appearance of a new car when the factory didn't want to run the car themselves. This was usually when the factory didn't have the time or the personnel to spare.

The car that raced in 1972 had the 'Daytona' bodywork, with four rows of cooling slots in the spare wheel cover being particularly apparent. The slots allowed hot air from the front-mounted radiator to exit over the car rather than back through the driver's compartment. Front and rear bumpers were removed and a small curved air-dam was fitted under the nose. Two rectangular auxiliary spot-lights were mounted, one each side of the radiator opening, and on the rear wing, at the opposite side to normal, a quick-release racing filler cap was fitted. The drivers for the twenty-four hours were Laffeach and Doncieux who finished seventeenth in the red Dino with its white-blue-white NART stripes. Although the 246 Dino did not appear in the 24-hour race again the connection between the road cars and Ferrari's racing cars had been restated.

Any further developments in the Dino story ended in 1972 because Ferrari were concentrating on its replacement, the 308GT4, although production continued until 1974. So, the question is, what did Ferrari achieve by producing the Dino, and was it a success? Undoubtedly the Dino's greatest success was in providing the Ferrari experience to a much wider sports car buying public. Its price was comparable with that of the Porsche 911S, and although its performance was slightly inferior the Dino's better looks and superior handling/roadholding resulted in a demand that could

only be spelt s-u-c-c-e-s-s. The Dino also created increased interest in the name Ferrari as a marque. Motoring magazines and periodicals from Italy to Australia road-tested and wrote about this new Ferrari. *Autocar* commented that in the previous ten years they had tested only four Ferraris, and their experience was no different from that of many other magazines, but all that changed with the appearance of the Dino Even the ordinary motorist in the street now appreciated that Ferrari made road cars, and not just racing cars.

In retrospect it would appear that Ferrari would not be in its present strong position without the production of the Dino and the effect it had on Ferrari/Fiat relations. In the Ferrari story it was definitely more than just another sports car.

EVOLUTION

Very few things in Ferrari history are straightforward, and so occasionally throughout this section you will see this sign?. This indicates that the information given is probable but not proved beyond all doubt. Chassis numbers are the main area of contention, because Ferrari are unable to confirm all the data. I am therefore grateful to fellow enthusiast Denny Schue for assistance with research.

1965: 'Dino Berlinetta Speciale' styling exercise on a racing Dino chassis appears at Paris Motor Show. S/N 0840 with in-line engine. The car is a very low two-seater, finished in red, with a distinctive wide perspex headlight cover.

1966: 'Dino GT Berlinetta' appears on the Dino stand at Turin Motor Show. S/N 00106 has an in-line engine. Has definite Dino features.

1967: 'Dino Berlinetta Prototipo Competizione' styling exercise appears on S/N 034 at Frankfurt show. Extravagant design has gull-wing doors, and racing car style wings front and rear.

206GT prototype with transverse engine appears at Turin Show. S/N not known. Lack of quarter-lights distinguishes this from production model.

First production prototype appears, with S/N 10523.

1968: Production of 206GT begins with S/N 00102, bodies now built by Scaglietti.

1969: Production of 206GTs ends. Last known chassis is 00404. Total 206GTs built is 150?

246GT officially introduced at Turin Show. Earliest known chassis is 00400.

1970: Last first series 246 produced, believed to be chassis 01116. S/N 01118 is first second series car. These have bolt-on wheels and ATE brakes.

First right-hand drive 246 appears. S/N 01134, in October.

From S/N 01250 small changes are made to the front bumpers. Total production of 246s for the year is 351?

1971: S/N 02130 is last second series car built, S/N 02132 is the first third series car. USA version appears with anti-pollution equipment, S/N 02866. Total 830? 246GTs built.

1972: 246GTS version is introduced at the Geneva Motor Show. It has lift-out roof panel for open-air motoring, S/N not known. Earliest known GTS is 03408. First British GTS is 03688. First US GTS is 03762. A 246GT runs in Le Mans 24 hours race and finishes seventeenth, entered by NART Production equals 973? GTs, and 280? GTSs.

1973: Last US coupé built, S/N 06860. Last European GT, S/N 07486. 346? GTs and 681? GTSs built in total.

1974: Last British GT built, S/N 07650. The GTS ceases production also. Last known chassis were: European 07772, British 07778, US 08518. Total production 10? GTS, and 300? GTSs.

Production Totals

European cars	1750?
British cars	740?
American cars	1400?
First Series cars	357
Second series cars	507?
Third series cars	3019?

Ferrari Dino 206GT & 246GT/S 1967 – 1974

Manufacturer	Ferrari Automobili S.p.A. SEFAC, Casella Postale 589, 41100 Modena, Italy

Number made (approx)	206GT	150
	246GT	2650
	246GTS	1250

Mechanical layout All types are mid-engined, rear wheel drive.

Engine
Type All are 65 degree V6, with chain-driven, twin ohc per bank.
206GT has all alloy block/head.
246GT has iron block/alloy head.

	206GT	246GT
Capacity	1987cc	2418cc
Compression ratio	9.0:1	9.0:1
Bore/stroke	86 x 57mm	92.5 x 60mm
Power	180bhp @ 8000rpm	195bhp @ 7600rpm
Torque	138lbf ft @ 6500rpm	165lbf ft @ 5500rpm
Carburettors	3 x 40DCN14 Webers	3 x 40DCNF/7 Webers

Gearbox Five forward gears with synchromesh and one reverse

Gear ratios:

1st	4.424:1	3.075:1
2nd	2.588:1	2.117:1
3rd	1.897:1	1.524:1
4th	1.488:1	1.125:1
5th	1.132:1	0.857:1
rev.	3.267:1	2.667:1
final drive	3.423:1	3.625:1

	206GT	246GT
Chassis	Traditional oval tube frame with secondary frames front and rear.	
Suspension	Independent all round with unequal length wishbones, coil springs and telescopic shock absorbers.	
Steering	Rack and pinion	
Brakes	ventilated discs all round	
Front	10.6in	10.6in
Rear	10.0in	10.6in
Swept area	48.4 sq. in.	
Wheels	14 x 6^1/$_2$in bolt-on	14 x 6^1/$_2$in five-stud
Bodywork	aluminium	steel
Electrical system	Marelli Dinoplex electronic ignition, with coil system back-up.	

Dimensions

Length	163.3in (4150mm)	166.5in (4230mm)
Width	67.0in (1700mm)	67.0in (1700mm)
Height	43.9in (1115mm)	44.6in (1135mm)
Weight	1980lb (900kg)	2376 (1080kg)
Wheelbase	2280mm	2340mm
Front track	1425mm	1425mm
Rear track	1400mm	1400mm

Performance

Performance figures always vary depending on the conditons under which they were recorded, so if you see different figures in other publications don't be surprised.

0 – 50mph	5.6s	5.5s
0 – 60mph	7.5s	7.1s
0 – 70mph	9.8s	9.2s
0 – 80mph	12.2s	11.4s
0 – 90mph	15.3s	14.5s
0 – 100mph	19.2s	17.6s
0 – 120mph	30.6s	28.5s
Maximum	140.0mph	148.0mph

ROAD TESTS

ROAD TEST

FERRARI DINO 246GT

Perfection is an absolute quality found only in nature or that part of it we call genius: it is rarely applicable to the collection of compromises known as the motor car. Occasionally, however, we do test cars that closely approach perfection, missing it only in details of execution or performance. Into this rare category comes the 2.4-litre transverse mid-engined Ferrari Dino 246 GT.

It attains this elevated classification not only because its designers and stylists have got virtually all their sums right—it cannot be faulted in any area of importance—but because they have endowed it with two additional virtues. The first is beauty—at least in the eyes of everyone at *Motor* who beheld it. The second is the car's forgiving and controllable behaviour when its limit of adhesion is finally exceeded, an important advance for a mid-engined vehicle which has revived our wavering faith in the concept for roadgoing cars. But few drivers will ever manage to lose the Dino, for it has the tremendous grip characteristic of this configuration. Unlike some other mid-engined cars, however, it has adequate threequarter rear visibility (excellent everywhere else) and a boot which is as capacious as the airy cockpit. Such spaciousness follows from an overall length almost as great as that of the latest Ford Cortina, yet with an overall height of only 45in. Pininfarina's graceful styling contrives to make it look a tiny jewel of a car, as miniscule as is claimed in the sales literature.

Then there is the superb engine, the equally superb gearbox, the exceptionally comfortable ride, the excellent driving position and the well laid out controls. Perhaps the Dino's only significant fault is its fuel consumption, which is rather heavy for its performance; apart from this we had no more than one or two minor complaints about such matters as ventilation and the location of the instruments. Nor is the Dino an unattainable dream: you have to be rich to own one but you needn't be a millionaire, for it is the "cheap" Ferrari, costing only £5486 in Britain—it has been available in rhd form since October. At this price demand

should greatly exceed supply and the car constitutes formidable opposition to the Porsche 911S.

Performance and economy

The original transverse-engined Ferrari Dino announced at the 1967 Turin Show was powered by a 2-litre light alloy 65° V6 with four chain-driven overhead camshafts built by Fiat to a Ferrari design for the Dinos of both companies. Two years later this engine was replaced by another of the same configuration but with a cast-iron block and capacity increased to 2.4 litres; it is now built—again for both Dinos—by Ferrari at Maranello. For the Ferrari Dino it develops 195 (net) bhp—15 bhp more than does the Fiat Dino version—at no less than 7600 rpm, and 155.5 lb. ft. of torque at 5500 rpm.

Ignoring the choke lever between the seats we found that it always started easily from cold, as is usual with Weber carburetters (of which there are three) by simply depressing the throttle pedal a few times to make the accelerator pumps squirt neat petrol into the cylinders. Once started it idled easily and pulled without hesitation at once. To produce nearly 200 bhp from 2.4 litres the Ferrari engine has to be very highly tuned by production standards, yet it pulls extraordinarily well from low speeds. For demonstration purposes it can be made to do so from 1000 rpm in fifth by carefully feeding in the throttle, though if the pedal is floored at around 1500 rpm the engine will hesitate, maybe die. But from 1800 rpm onwards the engine pulls with real vigour, gathering particular strength at just under 3500 rpm and continuing to deliver a surge of power right up to the 7800 rpm limit—surely the highest of any car currently in series production. And throughout this rev range the engine is utterly smooth and unfussed, so much so that care must be exercised to prevent over-revving. All this to the accompaniment of a mellow baying from the four exhaust pipes combined with a whine from the camshaft chains and a faint excited gnashing from the valvegear. Everyone liked this exciting noise, but a few of our test staff thought it just a little too loud and found it tiring on long journeys, even though it reduces to a contented burble when cruising at 100-110 mph, at which speed there is very little wind noise provided the doors are properly shut—they need a good slam.

Despite the handicap of considerable weight for a sports car—23.3 cwt. unladen—and by absolute standards relatively modest capacity and power, the Dino is a very quick car. It gets to 60 mph from rest in 7.1 sec., to 100 mph in 17.6 sec. and will comfortably pull maximum revs in top gear giving a maximum speed of 148 mph. The engine is so torquey that this gear often feels lower than it actually is, inducing an initial underestimation of speed. The Dino's excellent performance in the upper part of the speed range follows largely from its excellent aerodynamics as demonstrated by its flat fuel consumption curve which remains comfortably above 20 mpg at 100 mph. The shape also has other important aerodynamic qualities, for the car feels impressively secure and stable at very high speeds and proved to be virtually impervious to side winds.

Most of our staff thought this Pininfarina design superb; certainly it was a head-turner wherever it went. Its most ingenious feature is the wrap-around rear window which gives adequate threequarter rear vision. Only the protruding door handles spoil the side view, though these may be necessary to avoid the ducts in the flanks supplying air to the carburetters and brakes

MOTOR week ending July 10 1971

Unfortunately the low drag factor does not seem to have counterbalanced the disadvantage of considerable weight—and perhaps of rich-running Webers—for the fuel consumption is rather poor and once or twice plunged below 15 mpg during particularly fast runs, though the final overall figure was 16.1 mpg of 5-star fuel. But owners will probably find, as we did, that after the novelty of the Dino's high performance has worn off, it is possible to get along almost as quickly as before with rather less use of the revs and gears; the fuel consumption then improves to the 17-19 mpg level, giving a range from the 15.5 gallon tank of around 260 miles.

Transmission

Following the Ferrari tradition there is a gate at the base of the Dino's floor-mounted gearlever to define the positions of the five speeds which are arranged Porsche-fashion: first and reverse are to the left of the upper four gears laid out in the usual H. No spring loading is used except for reverse, obtained with a downward push. At a casual glance the presence of the gate might seem to introduce navigational inhibitions, and indeed our testers did need a little practice to get used to the change from first to second. But after a time the presence of the gate

is forgotten and the first-second movement becomes as easy and natural—though perhaps a little slower—as, right from the start, do the movements between all the other gears. The gearbox then reveals itself as being superb with unobtrusive but effective synchromesh which allows lightning changes to be sliced through. The lightness and feeling of precision is remarkable in view of the distant location of the transmission behind and beneath the engine to which it is coupled by three spin gears.

On our test car, the quicker the changes the more easily they went through, as the rather heavy clutch did not always disengage completely when depressed. Like the throttle, however, it was very progressive in action so smooth changes are easy once the driver has allowed for the fact that although the engine revs rise quickly enough when the throttle is blipped, they tend to die slowly, perhaps because of a heavy flywheel.

Well-spaced maxima of 41 mph, 59 mph, 81 mph and 110 mph are possible in the four indirect gears. The engine's excellent

These three levers, below left, in the driver's door jamb unlock the front and rear compartments and petrol filler cap; the cockpit is spacious with plenty of legroom for tall drivers, but the seats are too small

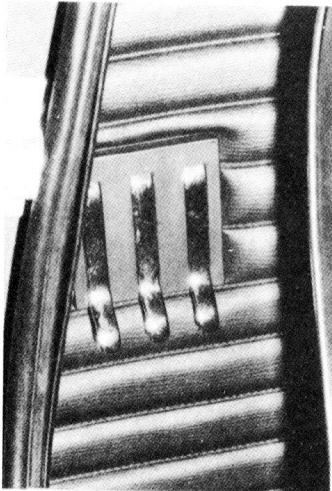

torque at low revs made it rarely necessary to use bottom gear for anything other than starting off. Only in fourth was some transmission whine audible.

Handling and brakes

When it comes to getting round corners the Ferrari Dino has all the advantages—and makes use of them. One such is racing-style double-wishbone suspension at both ends. Another is the location of the engine just behind the driver which puts more weight on the rear wheels for good traction in slippery conditions and less on the front wheels to allow the use of fat tyres with direct manual steering. Both these last two ends have in particular been admirably achieved on the Ferrari: it has monster 205 XVR Michelin radials guided at the front by superbly precise, direct steering which gives good feel with little kickback and is one of the joys of the car.

The inevitable result of all this is an ability to go round corners, which makes ordinary cars seem wholly inadequate. Only when trying a normal saloon after the Dino does a driver realize just how effortlessly and quickly he has been going. Terms like understeer and oversteer are generally pretty academic: the car just steers. Further acquaintance reveals that taking a corner

A gate is a traditional feature of a Ferrari gearchange, below; the transverse V6 fits snugly into its compartment behind the driver

MOTOR week ending July 10 1971

under power tends to create not so much gentle oversteer as a useful tightening of the line.

So much for impressions on the road—we needed the relative security of a closed test track to learn more about the Dino's phenomenally high limits. Unlike many mid-engined cars it does not always understeer with power, and oversteer without it. On fast bends the gentle oversteer tendency was confirmed; on slow bends we were able to make the front end plough outwards with power. Equally, a vicious bootful of throttle in second could break the tail away though in an easily catchable way.

But there is a much more important question to be answered. Even the Dino must run out of grip eventually—what happens when it does? For the practised anticipation and lightning responses of the professional racing driver, mid-engined cars may be fine, but with their centrally located masses they do tend to spin rapidly when all is finally lost, an unsatisfactory characteristic for the more ordinary mortals likely to drive Dinos on the road, one that has made us hesitate to endorse the concept for practical roadgoing sports cars.

Such hesitations are swept aside by the forgiving nature of the Dino. To begin with, helped by a limited-slip differential, it retains a large measure of its traction and cornering power in the wet, though it does have one vice: a tendency to plane outwards at the front on puddles and rivulets perhaps a little more than would a front-engined car. But if you lift your foot sharply off the accelerator in a corner the car responds with nothing more than a slight twitch that calls for little steering correction. Even if this is done when cornering nearly on the limit, the tail breaks away in a gentle and controllable way, a response to which we had reason to feel gratitude as fuel surge tended to make our test car cut out when entering a corner under the combination of deceleration and turning. It is this safe behaviour in extreme conditions that makes the Dino so outstanding.

To match this handling are brakes of equal calibre. The four huge outboard ventilated discs are operated with servo assistance through a front/rear split hydraulic system. Surprisingly, in view of the 43/57 front/rear weight distribution, there is a pressure relief valve in the rear line, showing how much weight can be transferred to the front wheels during heavy braking. In mid-engined cars this may not be enough to prevent front wheel lock up under heavy braking—especially in the wet—but of this vice the Dino was completely free. Though the pressures required were rather higher than is usual nowadays—the maximum 1g deceleration being achieved with a force of 135lb—the brakes felt immensely progressive and reassuring in their action. As might be expected from their racing heritage, they did not fade either on the road or during our test, nor were they affected by a thorough soaking in the watersplash. But a really strenuous pull on the handbrake gave a deceleration of no more than 0.31g.

Comfort and controls

Few saloon cars other than Citroens—let alone sports cars—ride better than the Dino Firm, rather than harsh at low speeds, the suspension simply smothers the biggest

Motor road test No. 30/71 — Dino Ferrari 246GT

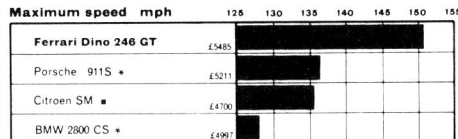

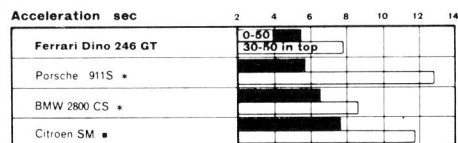

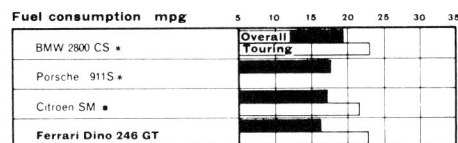

Maximum speed mph

		125	130	135	140	145	150	155
Ferrari Dino 246 GT	£5485							
Porsche 911S *	£5211							
Citroen SM ∎	£4700							
BMW 2800 CS *	£4997							

Acceleration sec

		2	4	6	8	10	12	14
Ferrari Dino 246 GT	0-60 / 30-50 in top							
Porsche 911S *								
BMW 2800 CS *								
Citroen SM ∎								

Fuel consumption mpg

	5	10	15	20	25	30	35
BMW 2800 CS *	Overall / Touring						
Porsche 911S *							
Citroen SM ∎							
Ferrari Dino 246 GT							

* obsolete models
∎ estimated

Make: Ferrari. Model: Dino 246GT. **Makers:** Ferrari Automobili S.p.A. SEFAC, casella postale 589, 41100 Modena, Italy. **Concessionaires:** Maranello Concessionaires Ltd, Egham-by-pass, Surrey. **Price:** £4,200 plus £1,285.63 purchase tax equals £5,485.63. Electric window lifters £83.55 extra with tax

Performance tests carried out by *Motor's* **staff at the Motor Industry Research Association proving ground, Lindley.**

Test Data: World copyright reserved; no unauthorised reproduction in whole or in part.

Conditions

Weather: Warm and dry
Temperature: 64-68°F
Barometer: 29.85 in Hg
Surface: Dry concrete
Fuel: 101 octane (RM) 5-star rating

Maximum Speeds

		mph	kph
Max. speed		148	238
4th gear		110	177
3rd gear	at 7,800	81	130
2nd gear	rpm	59	95
1st gear		41	66

Acceleration Times

mph		sec.
0-30		2.6
0-40		3.6
0-50		5.5
0-60		7.1
0-70		9.2
0-80		11.4
0-90		14.5
0-100		17.6
0-110		22.0
0-120		28.5
Standing quarter mile		15.4
Standing kilometre		27.8

mph	Top sec.	4th sec.	3rd sec.
10-30	—	—	5.2
20-40	8.4	6.0	3.6
30-50	7.8	5.0	3.3
40-60	7.8	4.5	3.6
50-70	7.2	5.3	3.6
60-80	7.3	5.4	4.1
70-90	8.2	5.5	—
80-100	8.9	6.2	—
90-110	9.5	7.2	—
100-120	11.8	—	—

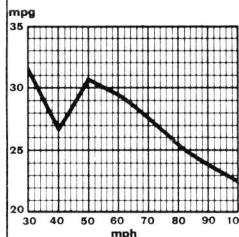

mpg

Fuel Consumption

Touring (consumption midway between 30 mph and maximum less 5% allowance for acceleration) . . . . 23.0 mpg
Overall . . . . 16.1 mpg
(= 17.5 litres/100km)
Total test distance . . . 1,294 miles

Brakes

Pedal pressure, deceleration and equivalent stopping distance from 30 mph

lb.	g.	ft.
25	0.34	88
50	0.71	42
75	0.86	35
1-0	0.92	33
135	0.98	31
Handbrake	0.31	97

Fade Test

20 stops at ½g deceleration at 1 min. intervals from a speed midway between 40 mph and maximum speed (=95.5 mph)

		lb.
Pedal force at beginning	. . . .	35
Pedal force at 10th stop	. . . .	35
Pedal force at 20th stop	. . . .	35

Steering

		ft.
Turning circle between kerbs:		
Left	. . . .	37
Right	. . . .	36
Turns of steering wheel from lock to lock	. . . .	3.1
Steering wheel deflection for 50ft. diameter circle	. . . .	1.25 turns

Clutch

Free pedal movement = ½in.
Additional movement to disengage clutch completely = 2½in.
Maximum pedal load = 43lb.

Speedometer

Indicated	10	20	30	40	50	60	70
True	10	19	27	37½	47½	57½	67½
Indicated	80	90	100				
True	77	87	97				

Distance recorder 3% fast

Weight

Kerb weight (unladen with fuel for approximately 50 miles) 23.3 cwt.
Front/rear distribution . . 43/57
Weight laden as tested . . 27.1 cwt.

MOTOR week ending July 10 1971

Motor road test No. 30/71 Dino Ferrari 246GT

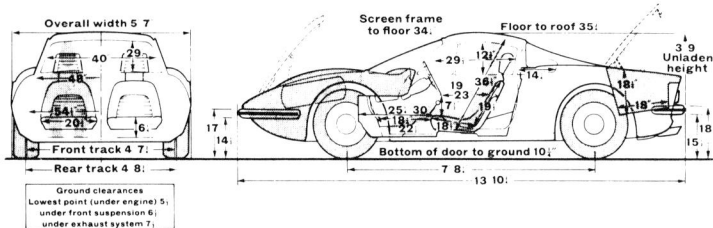

Overall width 5 7

Screen frame to floor 34.

Floor to roof 35:

3 9 Unladen height

Front track 4 7:

Rear track 4 8:

17 1 14:

18.

15.

Bottom of door to ground 10¼

7 8.

13 10:

Ground clearances
Lowest point (under engine) 5¼
under front suspension 6¼
under exhaust system 7¼

Engine
Block material	Light alloy
Head material	Light alloy
Cylinders	6 in V
Cooling system	water
Bore and stroke	92.5mm (3.64in.) 60mm (2.36in.)
Cubic capacity	2418 cc (148.1 cu.in)
Main bearings	4
Valves	Dohc
Compression ratio	9.0:1
Carburetters	Three Weber 40DCN F/7
Fuel pumps	Two Bendix electric
Oil Filter	Full flow
Max. power (net)	195 bhp at 7600 rpm
Max. torque (net)	165·5lb.ft. at 5500 rpm

Transmission
Clutch sdp diaphragm mechanically operated

Internal gearbox ratios
Top gear	0.857:1
4th gear	1.125:1
3rd gear	1.524:1
2nd gear	2.117:1
1st gear	3.075:1
Reverse	2.667:1
Synchromesh	All forward ratios

Final drive 4.44:1 spur transfer gears
Mph at 1,000 r.p.m. in:—
Top gear	19.0
4th gear	14.1
3rd gear	10.4
2nd gear	7.5
1st gear	5.2

Chassis and body
Construction . . . . . Steel tubular and sheet construction with aluminium body panels.

Brakes
Type . . Servo assisted ventilated discs operated by split hydraulic system with pressure relief valve in rear line.
Dimensions 10.6in. dia., front and rear

Suspension and steering
Front	Independent by wishbones with coil springs and an anti-roll bar
Rear	Independent by wishbones with coil springs and an anti-roll bar

Shock absorbers:
Front } Telescopic, double-acting Konis
Rear }
Steering type	Cam gears rack and pinion
Tyres	205/70 VR 14X Michelin
Wheels	14in.
Rim size	6½ in.

Coachwork and equipment
Starting handle	No
Tool kit contents	Reflective triangle, jack, brace, pliers, Philips and ordinary screwdrivers, plug, carburetter and open-ended spanners.
Jack	Screw pillar
Jacking points	One each side
Battery 12 volt	negative earth 60 amp hrs capacity
Number of electrical fuses	12
Headlamps	Halogen type
Indicators	Self-cancelling flashers
Reversing lamps	Yes
Screen wipers	Electric, self-parking, variable speed
Screen washers	Electric
Sun visors	Two

Locks:	
With ignition key	Doors
Interior heater	Fresh air
Upholstery:	
Floor covering	Carpets
Alternative body styles	None
Major extras available	Electric window lifters

Maintenance
Fuel tank capacity	15.5 galls
Sump	12 pints SAE 10W30
Gearbox and final drive	8 pints SAE EP80
Steering gear	035 Shell Spirax EP90
Coolant	30 (2 drain taps)
Chassis lubrication	Every 3000 miles to 4 points
Maximum service interval	3000 miles
Ignition timing	6° btdc
Contact breaker gap	0.012-0.015in.
Sparking plug gap	0.16-0.20in
Sparking plug type	Champion N60Y
Tappet clearance (cold)	Inlet 0.00 7/in Exhaust 0.017/in

Valve timing:
inlet opens	40° btdc
inlet closes	52° abdc
exhaust opens	53° bbdc
exhaust closes	31° atdc
Rear wheel toe-in	⅛ in.
Rear wheel camber	0° 50′ ± 1° 15′
Front wheel toe-in	⅛ in.
Camber angle	0° + 15′
Castor angle	4°
King pin inclination	9° 3′

Tyre pressures:
Front	27 psi
Rear	31 psi

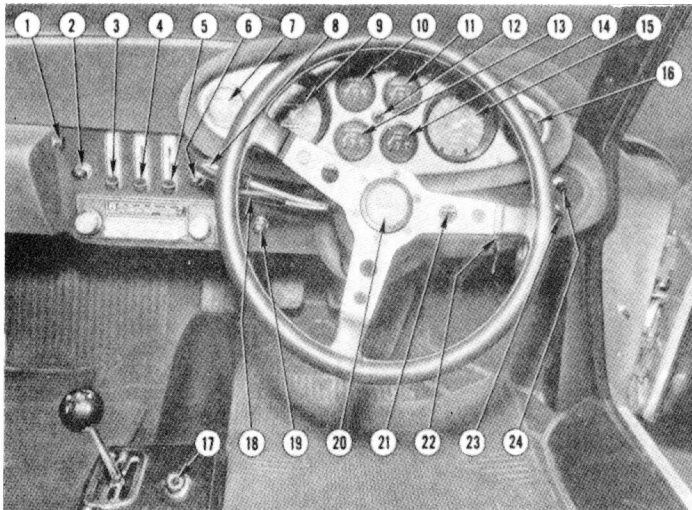

1 glovebox catch. 2 footwell fan. 3 left-hand heater distribution control. 4 heater temperature. 5 right-hand heater distribution control. 6 screen fan. 7 ammeter. 8 lights stalk. 9 speedometer incorporating trip and total mileometers. 10 oil temperature gauge. 11 water temperature gauge. 12 trip zero. 13 oil pressure gauge. 14 fuel gauge. 15 rev counter. 16 clock. 17 cigarette lighter. 18 indicator stalk. 19 hazard warning switch. 20 horn button. 21 wash/wipe stalk. 22 ignition lock. 23 instrument lighting rheostat. 24 wipers rheostat.

bumps and soaks up undulations without pitch, float or bottoming. The comfort provided contributes greatly to the feeling of security so characteristic of the car. Unfortunately, the ride is not matched by the seats, which could only suit midgets and have rolls across the tops of their backrests which dug into the shoulder blades of even our shortest drivers. These backrests incorporate adjustable headrests but do not recline—there wouldn't be room for them to do so anyway. In partial compensation for these defects the range of fore-and-aft adjustment is enough to satisfy the legroom requirements of human beings at the other extreme of size as represented by our resident 6ft. 5in. giant. And the seats do provide good lateral support, helped by the rest for the left foot which constitutes an excellent bracing spot.

Sports cars tend to have cramped cockpits; Italian cars to have the steering wheel too far away and the pedals too close. Though the Dino is both sporting and Italian, its small steering wheel (which has a leather-covered rim) and its pedals are so well located that everyone was able to achieve a comfortable driving position, regardless of size. Gearlever and handbrake, too, could be reached without effort by all our test staff when wearing seatbelts. Fingertip control over all the services completes the feeling of unity with the machine that the Dino imparts. On the left there is an indicator stalk with behind it a longer stalk controlling all the modes of side and headlamp operation, while in conformity with another of our preferences the horn is operated by a button at the centre of the wheel. A right-hand stalk controls the washers and the wipers which have no intermittent action but can be varied in speed by a rheostat mounted on the facia near the stalk. The wiper arms have an overlapping "clap hands" action which allows them to clear the screen close to both edges, though the wiped area should extend further up the screen for tall drivers. These arms also accelerate as they move from their central positions and even at their lowest speeds make a loud and wearing thump as they contact the frame at the sides of the windscreen. At medium to fast speeds they flick over the frame completely and can be seen through the quarterlights.

The deep, wide and steeply raked screen gives excellent forward visibility over the low bonnet. This falls away towards the ground between the wheelarches out of the driver's sight so that there is more car in front than is at first realized, calling for extra care during parking manoeuvres. In contrast the blunt Kamm-type tail is easily seen from the cockpit. It is seen through the rear window which is one of the Dino's most striking features; nearly vertical and no more then 8 in. high, it curls backwards through 90° at each end to meet the rear quarterlights set into the flanks of the car. In this way it provides a fair measure of the important three-quarter rear vision so lacking in some mid-engined designs while helping to isolate the occupants from engine noise, and in its protected location at the forward end of the rear deck, remains virtually untouched by dirt or rain. At night the halogen headlamps were good both when dipped and when on main beam so long as their plastic covers were kept clean.

There is virtually no wind noise below

MOTOR week ending July 10 1971

The rear boot (above) took 5.6 cu. ft. of our suitcases, which makes it capacious for a sports car. The toolkit lives in the front boot together with the spare wheel, jack etc. All switches and levers (below left) terminate in the same spatulate ends. In the boots lives the transistorized ignition system with a spare coil

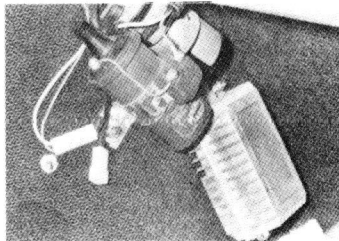

100 mph—it builds up gradually thereafter. Road noise is moderate despite the tautness of the steering and suspension which suggests minimum compliance. Radial tyres notwithstanding, it is more high-frequency roar than low-frequency thump.

Hot and cold air is admitted into the interior through four swivelling "egg-slicer" vents, two in the footwells and two on the facia, close to the screen but a long way from the occupants. These are controlled by independent distribution levers for each side of the car which flank a central temperature control lever. This is progressive in action but without the two booster fans (one for the footwells and one for the screen) the throughput is small. With the heater shut off, the screen booster provided just enough cool air in town for the warmish days of our test, and the volume can be increased

without introducing much extra noise at speed by winding the side windows down a little.

Fittings and furniture

Betraying a desire to match the graceful exterior and the curved plan-form of the windscreen—which is delineated by the deep shelf of the facia—the stylists have given the cowled instrument cluster an elliptical shape. Like the facia it is covered with a black velvety material. Neither the shape nor the material were popular with our staff despite their functional attributes in minimising obstruction to the base of the screen and in eliminating unwanted reflections. Less popular still were the locations of the speedometer and rev counter towards the ends of the major axis of their elliptical enclosure, just where they are dangerously obscured by the wheel rim to all but very short drivers—dangerous because the engine is so smooth and unfussed that even its very high 7800 rpm limit could easily be exceeded. On the other hand at no time did it show the slightest signs of rising temperature or falling oil pressure, yet the relevant gauges have been given pride of place, right in front of the driver.

Also covered in the velvety material, and retained by a cheap-looking catch but no lock, is the lid of the moderate-sized glove compartment. Together with the boxes built in to the doors this provides most of the oddments space, though there is room for small packets, newspapers and the like behind the seats. A vanity mirror in the passenger's sun visor, an ashtray and a cigarette lighter complete the cockpit fittings. The front compartment is filled by the spare wheel and toolkit, but the conventional rear boot is large for a sports car, taking 5.6 cu ft of our Revelation suitcases.

The Dino is very well equipped electrically. It has, for example, reversing lights, red warning lights in the door edges and lights for all three compartments. In the front compartment there are boxes of fuses each of which is clearly marked in three languages with the services it protects, while in the boot at the rear is the transistorized ignition system with its spare coil. Our test car was additionally fitted with the optional (£83.55 extra) electric window lifters.

Servicing and accessibility

When an engine is located in the centre of a car it is not easy to get at. The Ferrari's unit is not too bad in this respect except for the long dipstick which requires careful threading into its tube in the forward bank of cylinders under the hinged engine cover. Even minor repairs, however—like replacing blown exhaust gaskets—could prove expensive as the bulkhead in front of the engine cannot be removed so the complete engine/transmission unit may have to be removed for attention of this sort, though it is accessible through a removable panel at the rear of the boot and through detachable panels in the wheelarches.

Servicing, which includes some chassis greasing, is required every 3000 miles and there are 7 Ferrari dealers and distributors in the UK. There is a good toolkit which includes a reflective triangle, and an informative and well-illustrated three-language handbook. We found the pillar jack rather stiff in its action.

IRVING DOLIN PHOTOS

DINO 246 GT

Ferrari's version of the 6-cylinder business coupe

FERRARI'S JUNIOR CAR, the Dino, has taken so long to reach the U.S. market that it might look old-fashioned by now but for its handsome Pininfarina body. Named for Enzo Ferrari's deceased son Dino and derived from earlier racing cars carrying the same name, the first road-going Dino prototype appeared at the 1966 Turin show as the Dino 206GT. It was closely related to an earlier 2-liter racing car with its 1987-cc 65° V-6 engine residing amidship in a longitudinal position and driving a typical racing transaxle behind it. The engine with its light alloy block and heads, four overhead camshafts and three Weber carburetors also made its debut that year in another Dino: Fiat's production car of that name, an entirely different car with front engine and rear drive. Fiat produced these engines and they were tuned for 160 bhp vs the Ferrari's 180, but they shared their dimensions and basic design with the Ferrari unit.

The Dino shown at 1967's Turin show was better detailed and, more importantly, rearranged to provide more space for passengers and luggage. The engine had been turned 90° to become a "sidewinder" and now drove down from the clutch through a transfer drive to a gearbox located in its own casing under the sump. This car gave every indication of being a definitive production version; and indeed it was just that, as production began not long after that. When it did begin, Fiat produced the main engine parts but Ferrari did the assembling. And it should be noted that the production car, like the prototypes, did not carry

the *name* Ferrari. Dino is a separate make, as far as Ferrari is concerned.

At the 1969 Geneva show Ferrari showed an updated Dino with its engine displacement increased to 2418 cc by bore and stroke increases, power raised from 180 bhp @ 8000 rpm to 195 @ 7600, and name changed to 246GT to correspond with the new displacement. Since then there have been detail modifications to the gearbox, interior and exterior but the 246GT remains essentially the car it was at the 1967 Turin show: Ferrari's idea of a fullbore sporting 2-seater on a scale smaller than that of the 12-cylinder ⟶

COMPARISON DATA

	Dino 246GT	DeTomaso Pantera	Porsche 911E*
List price	$14,700	$9800	$8145
Curb weight, lb	2770	3155	2485
0-60 mph, sec	7.9	6.8	6.6
Standing ¼ mi, sec	15.9	14.5	15.4
Stopping distance from 80 mph, ft	273	325	273
Brake fade, 6 stops from 60 mph, %	nil	nil	nil
Cornering capability, g	0.836	0.782	0.732
Interior noise @ 70 mph, dbA	83	n.t.	78
Fuel economy, mpg	12.7	13.8	18.6

*5-speed gearbox

MAY 1972

DINO 246 GT

to supply fresh air to the exhaust ports, all the plumbing that goes with it, and an electromagnetic clutch that disengages the pump above 3500 rpm or so to minimize peak power loss. The safety and smog alterations to the car add to its weight and cost and detract from its performance: Coco Chinetti of Chinetti Motors, who loaned us our test car, estimates the price increase to be about $2000, and our test car weighed some 50 lb more than the European version. Peak power is cut about 10% by the smog equipment: throttle response and fuel economy undoubtedly are degraded too.

Mid-engine cars are reminiscent of early sports cars in that they usually make rather blatant sacrifices in habitability to achieve a very high level of roadholding. That sports cars offering great comfort, quiet operation, generous passenger space, etc. outnumber the more "ultimate" type today reflects the fact that today there is less need or justification for these sacrifices. Traffic conditions, speed limits and roads are such that cars of even moderately high capabilities can seldom be used to their limits. Yet it is a thrill to drive a car like the Dino, one whose capabilities are far beyond what even an expert driver can use in most real-world motoring, and that is the Dino's reason for being.

The Dino's most obvious sacrifice affects the human ear. It is noisy in the extreme. The sounds are exciting, to be sure: busy tappets, whining cam chains and transfer drive, a raucous exhaust system. All combine to give driver and

Ferraris, in price as well as specification.

It's not an easy job to conform such an exciting car to the American safety and smog regulations, and these are the reasons we had to wait so long for the Dino. This is the first published test of the U.S. version. Particularly difficult was modifying the high-output engine for 1972's federal emission limits: 80 net bhp per liter (that's 1.34 bhp/cu in. for English-system thinkers) is a lot for a road car in anybody's terms. Ferrari engineers tried fuel injection but were not satisfied, and they finally settled on the same solution applied to their 12s—an air injection pump

passenger sensations just short of those of a race car, and even on a slow run to the corner drugstore the Dino seems to be working, snarling, racing. The exhaust note at low speeds gives away its 6-cyl configuration, but as the engine climbs into its effective rev range (little happens below 3000 rpm, and the unit is decidedly unhappy at low speeds, bucking and misfiring to prove it) it takes on the characteristic Ferrari sounds despite having only half the number of cylinders.

For an extended trip in the Dino we'd recommend taking a pair of earplugs along. Above 65 mph everything smooths out and the wind noise is low, so the Dino is no noisier at 70 mph than a Capri V-6 is at 90. But between 50 and 65 mph (2600-3500 rpm in 5th) the exhaust system resonates badly in the body cavity and the interior is actually louder at 50 than at 70.

Running up through the gears is quite another thing; this is when we relish the sounds, and the potent V-6 hitting 7800 rpm, the redline, is real music. Zero-to-60-mph acceleration, however, is not the Dino's forte, as the somewhat disappointing time of 7.9 sec shows. We tested the car at Lime Rock, Connecticut, where a particularly grippy new track surface absolutely prevented wheelspin getting off the line. The alternative is to slip the clutch, which we did, but we were reluctant to slip it enough to hold the engine at its 5500-rpm torque peak for the first couple of seconds; thus the engine spent an inordinate amount of time in lower rev range on the 0-60 run. The clutch did take what punishment we dealt it with no complaint whatsoever, but in any case the Dino isn't as quick as its Porsche competition. No problem explaining why: with approximately the same displacement, it weighs nearly 300 lb more than the Porsche even in the latter's heavier Targa form.

Another common sacrifice in mid-engine cars is in gearshifting: so far it's been unusual to find satisfactory shift linkage in mid-engine cars and the Dino is no exception.

The 5-speed gearbox is behind the engine, which complicates things and is typical of midship layouts whether longitudinal or transverse. On the Dino the shift pattern puts 5th over to the left and back, the other four gears in H-pattern—like the earlier Porsche 911s. This is a good layout for road work in which 1st is seldom used, but in everyday driving it's most inconvenient. It's often difficult to get the recalcitrant, gated shifter into 1st and sometimes it didn't want to go from 4th to 5th either; the acceleration runs were further hampered by the necessity of quite deliberate motion to get from 1st to 2nd.

A manual choke gave almost instantaneous cold starts at ambient temperatures around 30°F during our test, and the engine would restart quickly when hot when the accelerator pedal was held all the way down while cranking. There's always a backfire or two after shutting off, just to remind us of that air injection, and an additional symptom of the emission control is a very slow return to idle.

If engine behavior isn't the most exhilarating thing about the Dino, then its chassis is; the real joy of a good mid-engine car is in its handling and braking and the Dino shone as we expected it to. The steering is light, wonderfully precise and quick without being super-quick in the sense of the Citroen SM, and it transmits by what seems a carefully planned amount of feedback exactly what is going on at the tires. Thanks to the layout's low polar moment of inertia, the car responds instantly to it. The Dino's cornering limits are very high and we thoroughly enjoyed lap after lap at Lime Rock, finding its limits and improving our times. Though the sharpest lefthand turn brought on some fuel starvation, all was well otherwise and even if the throttle foot was lifted in the middle of an overdone turn, the only consequence was a gently drifting tail. A bumpy surface, of which there are many in rural New England, revealed even more: it takes a big disturbance to upset the Dino's equilibrium.

--->

DINO 246 GT

Braking is just as good, as the stopping distance of 140 ft from 60 mph indicates. An anchors-out stop may lock the front wheels, but the stopping power is simply phenomenal and should impart enough confidence that any driver will be able to modulate pedal effort and unlock them. Only one detraction from this impressive brake performance, achieved with big ventilated discs all around: in light, low-speed braking one notices a bit of nonlinearity in the vacuum booster's action.

Rough road surfaces also bring out a finely engineered ride. Despite being a very low car the Dino has plenty of suspension travel (those wheel arches mean something!) and other than a creak from the left rear suspension the car was at home on any paved road surface we subjected it to. The body also feels strong and solid, but the only way to tell if it's squeaking or rattling is to throw out the clutch and let the engine idle. It is, as it turns out, creaking a bit but the engine and drivetrain din covers this completely.

Seating is another area of mid-engine compromise and the Dino comes off better than most in this respect. Headroom isn't what you'd call generous, but a male of average height can sit comfortably, the big windshield doesn't brush his forehead, and he can see out—even to the rear, where the concave wraparound window is a good solution to a problem that is seldom well solved. The driver's legs necessarily aim toward the car center because of intruding wheelwells. Seatbacks are not adjustable and the seats don't rock on their mountings, but there is adequate fore-aft travel for a fair range of drivers and the brake and throttle pedals are well positioned for simultaneous use.

Some aspects of the ergonomics design are crude. Though a nice set of instruments is set into a panel right in front of the driver, the steering-wheel rim obscures the speedometer (which clicked loudly despite an attempt at repairs) badly. And that otherwise satisfactory rear window's center section reflects whatever is seen through the windshield, quite a problem at night. Heater controls are confusing, even after careful study of the owner's manual which, wonder of wonders, is a trilingual affair with very good specifications tables, drawings, photographs and minor service instructions. The heater has only a 1-speed blower; but its fresh-air intake is good and heat output powerful.

The Dino's interior, in standard form, is nicely put together but not fancy: about the grade of a Fiat 124 Spider. Leather can be ordered for $275 extra, cloth seat inserts for $65. Our test car had the standard all-vinyl coverings.

Ironically, this Dino was our first exposure to full results of the new 1972 seatbelt regulation, which requires a visual or audible warning if the ignition is on, the handbrake off and the transmission in gear, and if the passenger seat is occupied, without the belts being fastened. It sounds terrible but is actually little bother to those already in the habit of using belts. If you fasten the belt before putting the car in gear (which is natural anyway) you'll never hear the buzzer or see the light. As for your passenger, it can help get her or him to use the belts.

The transverse engine allows a sizable, usable trunk—6.7 cu ft, larger than a Camaro's—and it is nicely finished with carpeting on five of its six surfaces. The spare tire, quite a bulky thing, lives up front behind the radiator. Fuel is stored in two "saddlebag" tanks flanking the engine and fed by a single filler. Clever space utilization is what makes the Dino such a satisfactory mid-engine package.

Ferrari name or no, the Dino is a Ferrari and the mystique plus the exciting shape plus the sounds plus the great chassis all add up to a lot of car. Looking at it another way, in direct comparison to the Porsche 911E or S, it's difficult to justify the Dino's extra cost because the Dino isn't as quick, doesn't shift as well, uses more fuel, and offers less passenger space. Only in handling does it have a clear advantage over the Stuttgarter and this is akin to comparing a New York steak to a Spencer—both are very good but one is just a bit better.

The conclusion? If you must have a mid-engine car, you can do a lot worse than the Dino. But don't expect to wallop your neighbor's 911S with it.

ROAD TEST
DINO 246 GT

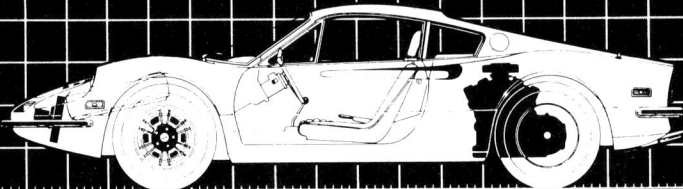

SCALE: 10" DIVISIONS

PRICE

List price, east coast $14,500
List price, west coast $13,885
Price as tested, east coast $14,740
  Price as tested includes electric
  windows ($240), dealer prep

IMPORTER

Chinetti Motors, Greenwich, Conn.
Modern Classic Motors, Reno, Nev.

ENGINE

Type	dohc V-6
Bore x stroke, mm	92.5 x 60.0
Equivalent in	3.64 x 2.36
Displacement, cc/cu in	2418/145
Compression ratio	9.0:1
Bhp @ rpm, net est.	175 @ 7000
Equivalent mph	127
Torque @ rpm, lb-ft est.	160 @ 5500
Equivalent mph	100
Carburetion	three Weber 40DCF14
Fuel requirement	premium, 98-oct

Emissions, gram/mile:

Hydrocarbons	3.25
Carbon Monoxide	22.68
Nitrogen Oxides	n.a.

DRIVE TRAIN

Transmission .... 5-sp manual
Gear ratios: 5th (1.05) 3.80:1

4th (1.38)	5.01:1
3rd (1.86)	6.75:1
2nd (2.59)	9.38:1
1st (3.76)	13.65:1
Final drive ratio	3.62:1

CHASSIS & BODY

Layout .... midship engine/rear drive
Body/frame.... unit steel, all steel panels
Brake system .... vented disc, 10.6-in front & 10.0-in rear; vacuum assisted
Swept area, sq in .... n.a.
Wheels .... cast alloy, 14 x 6½
Tires...Michelin XVR 205/70-VR14
Steering type ...... rack & pinion
  Turns, lock-to-lock 3.2
  Turning circle, ft 37.5
Front suspension: unequal-length A-arms, coil springs, tube shocks, anti-roll bar
Rear suspension: unequal-length A-arms, coil springs, tube shocks, anti-roll bar

ACCOMMODATION

Seating capacity, persons	2
Seat width	2 x 20.5
Head room, front/rear	35.5
Seat back adjustment, degrees	0

INSTRUMENTATION

Instruments: 170-mph speedo, 99,999 odo, 999.9 trip odo, 10,000-rpm tach, oil press, oil temp, water temp, ammeter, fuel level, clock
Warning lights: oil press, brake failure, low fuel, lights on, high beam, directionals, hazard flasher, seatbelts

MAINTENANCE

Service intervals, mi:

Oil change	6000
Filter change	6000
Gearbox & diff oil	6000
Minor tuneup	3000
Major tuneup	6000
Warranty, mo/mi	12/12,000

GENERAL

Curb weight, lb	2770
Test weight	3100
Weight distribution (with driver), front/rear, %	41/59
Wheelbase, in	92.1
Track, front/rear	56.2/56.3
Length	165.4
Width	67.0
Height	44.6
Ground clearance	4.7
Overhang, front/rear	40.3/33.0
Usable trunk space, cu ft	6.7
Fuel capacity, U.S. gal	18.6

CALCULATED DATA

Lb/bhp (test weight)	15.9
Mph/1000 rpm (5th gear)	18.2
Engine revs/mi (60 mph)	3200
Piston travel, ft/mi	1260
R&T steering index	1.20
Brake swept area, sq in/ton	n.a.

RELIABILITY

From R&T Owner Surveys the average number of trouble areas for all models surveyed is 11. As owners of earlier-model Ferraris reported 7 trouble areas, we expect the reliability of the Dino 246GT to be better than average.

ROAD TEST RESULTS

ACCELERATION

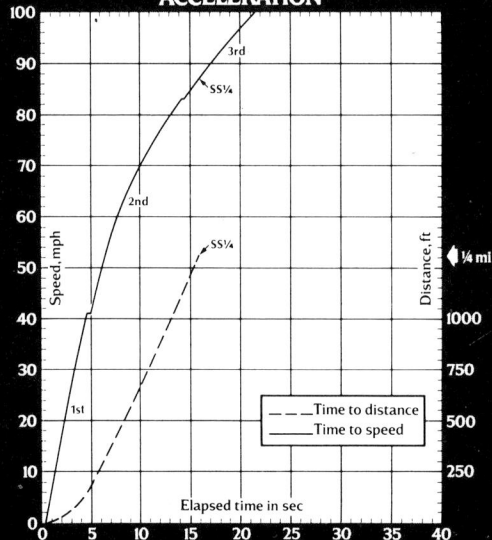

Time to distance, sec:

0-100 ft	3.2
0-500 ft	8.5
0-1320 ft (¼ mi)	15.9
Speed at end of ¼-mi, mph	87

Time to speed, sec:

0-30 mph	3.3
0-40 mph	4.5
0-50 mph	6.2
0-60 mph	7.9
0-70 mph	10.1
0-80 mph	13.1
0-100 mph	21.5

FUEL ECONOMY

Normal driving, mpg	12.7
Cruising range, mi (1-gal. res.)	224

SPEEDS IN GEARS

5th gear (7800 rpm)	141
4th (7800)	112
3rd (7800)	83
2nd (7800)	61
1st (7800)	41

BRAKES

Minimum stopping distances, ft:

From 60 mph	140
From 80 mph	273
Control in panic stop	very good
Pedal effort for 0.5g stop, lb	33

Fade: percent increase in pedal effort to maintain 0.5g deceleration in 6 stops from 60 ...... nil
Overall brake rating ...... very good

HANDLING

Speed on 100-ft radius, mph	35.4
Lateral acceleration, g	0.836

INTERIOR NOISE

All noise readings in dBA:

Idle in neutral	67
Maximum, 1st gear	89
Constant 30 mph	77
50 mph	85
70 mph	83
90 mph	86

SPEEDOMETER ERROR

30 mph indicated is actually	29.0
70 mph	66.5
80 mph	76.0

ACCELERATION

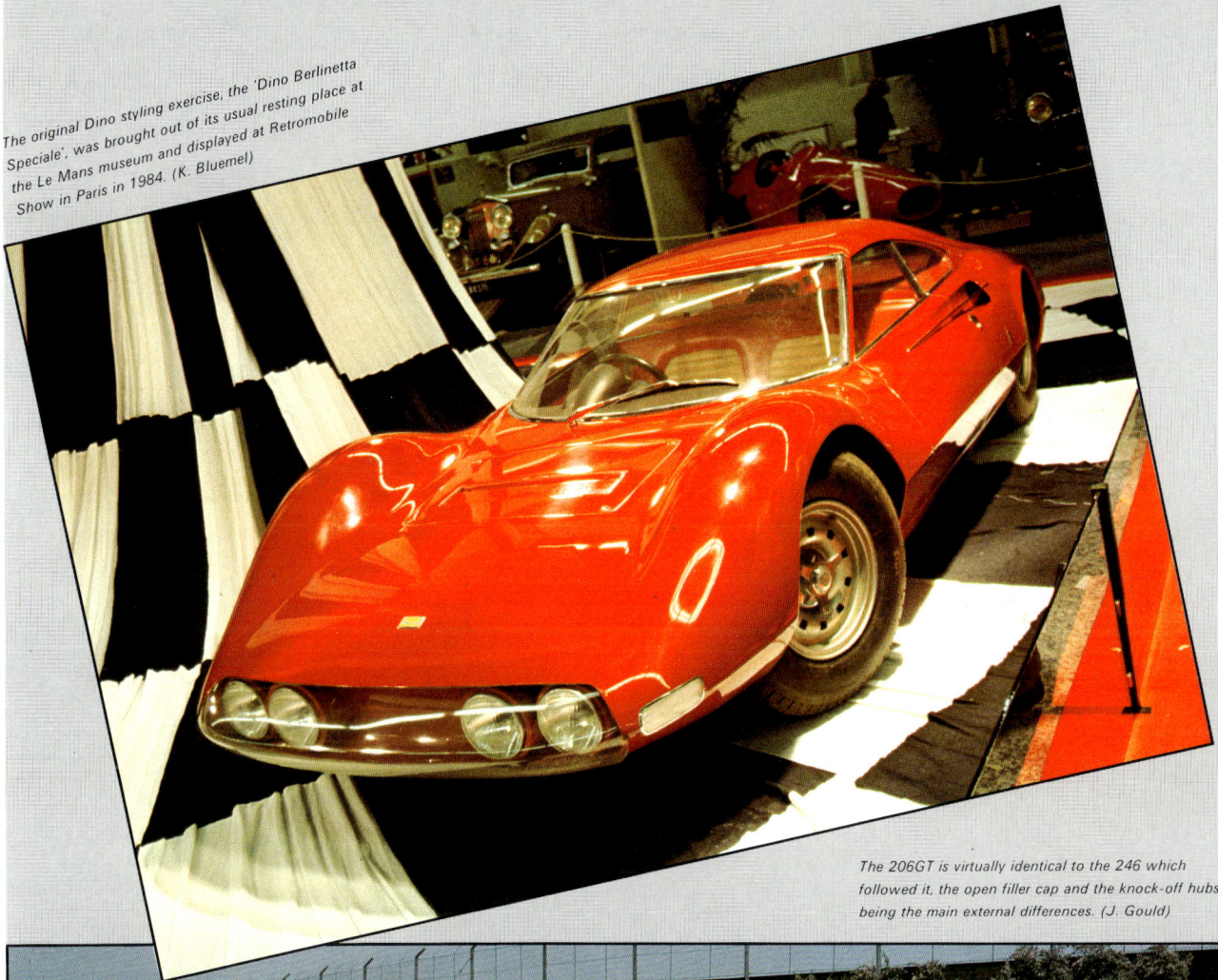

The original Dino styling exercise, the 'Dino Berlinetta Speciale', was brought out of its usual resting place at the Le Mans museum and displayed at Retromobile Show in Paris in 1984. (K. Bluemel)

The 206GT is virtually identical to the 246 which followed it, the open filler cap and the knock-off hubs being the main external differences. (J. Gould)

Above left: *Ferrari 206SP was the basis for the first Dino styling exercise, and shows similarities to production 206GT and 246GT, especially waistline and rear sail panel treatment. (K. Bluemel)*

Above right: *Road car follows race car style but within practical constraints, the cockpit area being noticeably wider.*

Main photo: *Flowing lines are typical Pininfarina and are very successful in making the Dino appear smaller than it actually is. The side profile highlights the elongated scoop feeding air to engine and brakes. Scoop is reminiscent of P3/P4 series of sports racing cars. (author)*

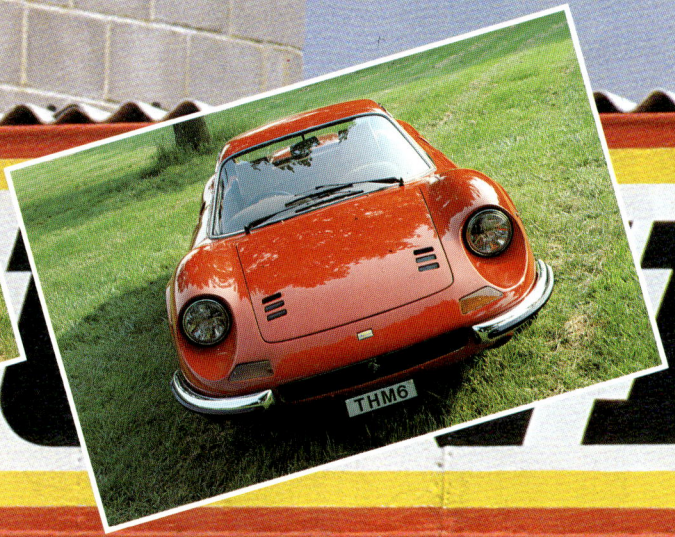

Above left: *The sills are low and entry is fairly easy but seats are low so one tends to drop into rather than sit in a Dino. The open hatches cover the engine and luggage compartment. (author)*

Above right: *From this angle the Dino looks deceptively diminutive; just don't try driving through a 5ft 6in gap! (author)*

The extended wheel arch flares apparent on this 'Daytona' Dino are necessary to cover extra rubber, but spoil the smooth lines of original design. (author)

The standard Dino wheel, and the wider Campagnolo wheel, of different design, fitted to the 'Daytona' Dino. The latter does not feature the 'Dino' badge.

Above left: This is a 246GT with 'Daytona package'.

Below left: The 246GTS with removable 'targa' roof panel. The rear sail panels have three slots, instead of the side window of GT version, which mirror those in the engine and spare wheel covers. This GTS also has optional perspex headlight covers.

Roof panel in position gives GT-like comfort when on the move. Because of relative scarcity, the open-air attractions and, some say, improved lines, the GTS is the most sought after variant. (J. Gould)

Driver's view of symmetrical instrument panel shows how tachometer and speedometer are badly placed.

The standard Dino interior sports all-leather seats and toning vinyl trim.

Modified interiors, reflecting owners' tastes, are not unusual. Shown here is an example with cloth-trimmed seat inserts and modified centre console and a concours car that has been refitted throughout in beige leather. Note also the carpets which have leather insets with the famous 'prancing horse' embossed in them (author).

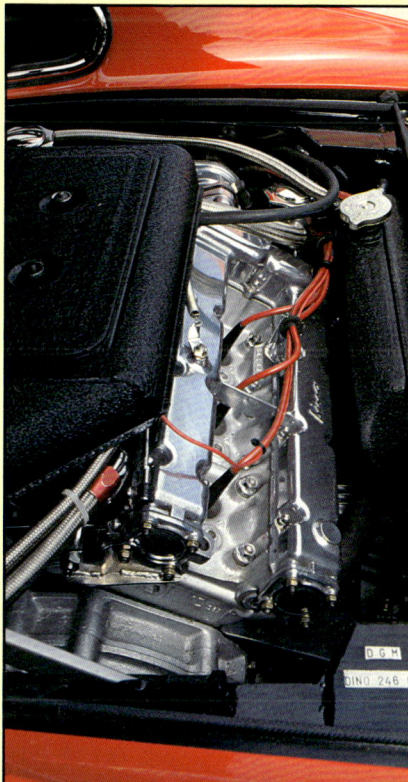

The heart of the Dino is the 2.4-litre V6 tucked in behind the seats. Note the Dino emblem on the cam cover. The engine, in fact, was manufactured not by Ferrari, but by Fiat.

Customising is not necessarily confined to the interior.
This heavily-modified Dino has extra wide wheels and
bumpers removed to save weight. (K. Bluemel)

Yet another area for modification. This engine has a fuel
injection system fitted for competition. (K. Bluemel)

The only Dino to race at Le Mans was entered by NART
in 1972. The car finished seventeenth overall. (LAT)

Owners' View

The two owners interviewed represent two differing ideologies, yet both undoubtedly treasure their Dinos. Terry Murphy is happy seeing his Dino sparkling and clean and being admired in a concours, while Jeff Simpson is happiest racing his Dino round Silverstone, or in some other speed event. As for the Dino, well it fits both of these roles equally well. Here then are Terry's and Jeff's views.

N.B. How did you become interested in the Ferrari Dino?

T.M. At the time I saw my first Dino I actually owned a Porsche 911S. About three weeks after I bought the Porsche I saw my first Dino and I thought 'I've got to have that red Dino'. The first thing that caught me was the styling, and also you don't have to know much about motor racing to know that Ferrari is a magic word, so I had to have one.

J.S. I think the Dino is a classic shape. To my mind it's a road-going version of the P3 racer, especially in spyder form, and it's a road development of the 206 competition car. Also when I bought it it's what I called a

half-price Ferrari, but which doesn't give half-price performance.

N.B. When did you first buy your Dino?

T.M. I bought it from a dealer in north London in 1976. I told my wife I was going out to buy a Volvo estate and came back with a Dino.

J.S. I bought the car twelve years ago, and I felt it was a car that I could use more regularly than one of the 12-cylinder Ferraris.

N.B. What condition was it in when you bought it?

T.M. It appeared to be good but the first service showed it needed a lot of work to put it right. There was a lot of body rust, which is common on Dinos.

J.S. The car was only two years old when I bought it so the body was in fairly good condition, but the main problem was with a faulty Dinoplex ignition which meant there was no rev counter, so a new Dinoplex had to be bought.

N.B. What repair or renovation work has been done?

T.M. Well, the body was stripped right down to bare metal, the sills were replaced, the wheel arches had to be done and the doors were reskinned. It was then resprayed Ferrari red. The original black vinyl interior was stripped out, and the whole interior retrimmed in beige leather. Then, in 1982, the engine blew up. I phoned Joe Nash at Dino Services who took it in to rebuild it. I told my wife there was something wrong with the electrics. I didn't dare tell her the engine had blown up or she would have divorced me (laughs). Now the car is like a brand new Ferrari, and I know exactly what's been done on it.

J.S. The replacement Dinoplex is still working well twelve years later, and since that time all I've had to do is replace the alternator bearings, water pump bearings and rebuild the distributor. Last year, at 60,000 miles I put a new clutch in it, but I don't think that's

bad. When I got the car I neutralised the rust and had it Waxoyled so any rust on it is only cosmetic.

N.B. Have you experienced difficulty in obtaining any parts?

T.M. Yes, wheels, and I would like to get a new set. Even though the wheels are repainted they seem to 'pit' a lot.

J.S. We had problems getting a Dinoplex, but part of the problem, in those days, was financial, but really we had no problems getting parts.

N.B. How do you feel about the performance and handling of the car?

T.M. It holds the road like a limpet. The brakes are excellent and instil the driver with confidence, and pull up dead straight, no problem at all. I've got the greatest confidence in it. Acceleration, braking and steering, I don't think there's anything to touch it.

J.S. The Dino is two cars. It's a road car, and for me, it's a competition car. As a road car it attracts a lot of attention so you tend to drive it very carefully, in case you attract boy-racers. I have run the car in Germany, on the autobahn, where it runs an indicated 155 mph, but I doubt if you can go much faster than 135 mph on the race track before the next bend comes up. On the track its handling is the best aspect. That and the braking. It's so well balanced. Mine is set up with a deal of understeer which gives a great feeling of security. It's easy to drive because, basically, the chassis can handle more power than the engine produces.

N.B. Do you use the car every day?

T.M. Not really. I only use it in the summer. It's not a practical car. When you drive it it's like a gas oven, it's that hot. The windows go up and down sometimes, and the horn works occassionally, but it's a Ferrari and you accept it.

J.S. It's not used every day. It needs to run at least ten miles just to warm the gearbox oil. The Dino now is of an age when it should be looked after and enjoyed rather than be used every day in city traffic.

N.B. Have you entered any concours and how did you fare?

T.M. In 1984 we had some super wins. Our greatest win was the championship at the Ferrari Owners Club. We won first in class at the Merton Pageant and a special commendation at the Bromley Classic and Sports car concours.

J.S. Well, there is a funny story, because it won a concours and the concours was then cancelled. It was a Ferrari Owners Club event which was ruined by torrential rain. My Dino was the only car in the class and so it won. I then had to pay the entry fee because I hadn't officially entered. But mine is not really a concours car.

N.B. Have you entered any motor sport events with the car?

T.M. I don't race it, although I did a few gentle laps of the Goodwood circuit a couple of years back.

J.S. I started racing the car four years ago, although it happened really by accident. I was living in Germany at the time, and a friend of mine who was living in Spain invited me to a Ferrari event at Mas du Clos in France. I went along as a spectator not knowing that he'd entered me into the competition, so I borrowed a crash hat, went out and won my class. Two weeks later there was a Dutch Ferrari Owners Club meeting at Zandvoort, so I went along and finished second in class, at a Grand Prix circuit. I was over the moon. I also had the unique experience of driving a ten lap race at the old Nürburgring, which I found very exciting. The same day I went to the Hockenheimring and entered a race there. I won an 'I love GTO' book at the Nürburgring, and another 'I love GTO' book at Hockenheim. I then returned to England, and invested in a set of

racing tyres, but the car remained otherwise totally standard. In 1985 I started to do hill-climbs as well as circuit races, and achieved some very satisfactory results.

N.B. As mentioned earlier, there is a Ferrari Owners Club, would you recommend people to join it?

T.M. Yes, I recommend all Ferrari owners to join. If I see someone with a Ferrari I always ask them if they are a member. If they are not I give them my phone number so I can give them the club address when they phone me. Other club members really make you welcome.

J.S. The Ferrari Owners Club consists of nearly a thousand people from all walks of life who come together and talk the same language. From that point of view the communication is superb between the people who own the cars, and one can find the best place for spare parts, servicing tips and the best people to service the car if you don't do it yourself. I think the cars get quite a lot of exposure through the efforts of the club, so I would say that it is essential to join the Ferrari Owners Club. If you don't own a Ferrari then join the Prancing Horse Register.

N.B. Is there a specialist whom you have found particularly useful?

T.M. There are a couple in fact. Joe Nash at Dino Services is the man to do my car, especially engine work. The other is Eddie Noon of Vale Cottage Motors. He takes great pride in his work.

J.S. I think there are body specialists and there are engine specialists and you wouldn't necessarily go to the same man to do both jobs. An exception to this

is Graypaul Motors, they do the whole job. Engine-wise I think Bob Houghton is in a position to give you more performance on a regular basis. Bodywork, I'm not really able to say, because I haven't had any done, except I know that Motor-tecnique are renowned for their panels and the work that they do on cars. David Cottingham does a very good job, and Terry Hoyle is an engine expert.

N.B. How would you sum up the enjoyment you get from your Dino?

T.M. Exhilarating! Every time I get in the car it's like driving it for the first time.

J.S. It gives me everything I need. What more could I want, it wins races, it wins hill-climbs, it turns people's heads when it's standing still. You can't replace a Dino.

N.B. What advise would you give to potential Dino owners?

T.M. To love it, and to look after it. It has to become part of your life.

J.S. Buy the most expensive Dino you can afford. Look at very many of them and compare Dino for Dino. The reason for paying as much as you possibly can is that the car will either already have been restored, or the car is original and you can judge how much work is needed to bring it up to the best spec possible.

BUYING

Buying

Although owning a Dino is a very attractive proposition, one should first of all give consideration to the type and amount of use it will have, because one thing is certain, it will be expensive to run. Only the wealthy could seriously consider a Dino for day-to-day transport, and even then the nagging doubts about its reliability might persuade one that a less exotic automobile would be a better choice. One has to remember that here is a car that needs a service every 3000 miles, and that Ferrari dealers charge a rather high rate per hour. Choosing to ignore the recommended service intervals is a false economy that will only result in even higher costs. Nevertheless if, having considered all the pros and cons, you decide to buy a Dino then what should you look for?

Well, one enthusiast's opinion is that if you want to buy a Ferrari then purchase the best one that is available, and pay the necessary high price. This should be a car for which the owner can produce evidence of regular servicing, and if necessary replacement

maintenance. If there is no evidence of regular servicing then look very, very carefully at all aspects of the car, because any work that subsequently shows itself to be necessary could prove to be prohibitively expensive. So look out for the following points.

Start by looking at the external appearance, and especially for any signs that indicate that the Italian disease, rust, is present. (Is it just a coincidence that rust is a four letter word?) On the Dino one needs to look closely at the sills, and the A-panels (the area just behind the front wheels). The wheel arches are another area where rust is a problem because dirt and mud collect there, and the rust eats its way through the bodywork from the inside, and eventually causes the paintwork to bubble. If the deterioration is caught before it becomes too widespread then the rotten part can be cut out and new pieces of metal shaped and inserted, but if a large area is affected then the only solution is to fit a complete new piece of bodywork. The nose and rear valance are also susceptible to stone chips, and if these are very deep then rust will also get a hold and spread underneath the paint. Whilst examining the bodywork also look for signs of repaired accident damage. This can show up as a rippled or uneven body panel, or a slight paint mismatch between two adjacent panels. The Dino's chassis is particularly strong and corrosion is not usually a problem, but the shock absorbers in the front suspension can give trouble. It's not unusual for them to rattle until they have warmed up, but if the car starts to wander on straight slightly uneven roads then this could indicate that it's time to replace them. Also listen for noise from the rear suspension which might mean that it's time to replace the bushes.

The brake system consists of hydraulically-operated ventilated discs all round, and the

adjustment mechanism on the rear calipers can cause problems. This can seize up, and results in the hand brake being non-operative, not that it's very good to start with. Whilst checking the adjustment on the calipers it is also a good idea to look at the discs for signs of scoring. If it's bad then they'll have to be replaced. The heart of any Ferrari is the engine, and although this one is only half a twelve it is still undoubtedly a Ferrari engine. There are, though, a couple of areas that need close scrutiny if one wants to avoid a very expensive trip to the workshop. Nearly all Dinos are subject to excessive wear on the camshaft lobes with the resulting expense of reprofiling or replacing. Regular tappet adjustment and replacing of the tappet pads is the only way to keep the camshafts in reasonable shape. Hence the recommendation that the car has a good service record. With four camshafts to replace in this department if anything is wrong it is worth while looking very closely for any signs of irregularities in the engine performance. Having said that, a well maintained unabused engine should run to a high mileage.

The engine is fed by three twin-choke Weber carburettors, and to keep the engine in tune properly these need to be set every three thousand miles.

Ferrari gearboxes are traditionally strong, but traditionally have weak syncromesh on second gear, and the Dino is no exception. Contrary to what one might think, the sign of a good gearbox is one that WON'T engage second gear until the gearbox is warm. If it goes into second when cold then something is wrong, it should only work when warm. When warmed-up check the condition of the gearbox by making a few quick changes up and down the box and especially through second. Also whilst we're talking about the rear of the car get underneath and have a look at the condition of the exhaust system. A replacement will be expensive.

Finally, the interior is one area to give a visual once-over. Worn carpets, split seats and even splits in the dashboard covering should be readily apparent, and obviously it is up to the buyer to decide if he likes what he sees, but again, it should be remembered that not inconsiderable expense will be incurred to rectify any problem in this area. Also give particular attention to the inner door panels, because if these are warped it will mean that damp, or water, is present. This usually happens because the water that runs down the windows goes straight into the doors and if the drain holes in the bottom of the doors have become blocked then the water can't get out. It can also cause the bottom of the doors to start rusting through.

Even so, the chances are that when you step out of the car, and look at that superb shape, and recall the performance that you've just experienced on a test drive, only the strongest willed will be able to take everything into

account. So having decided that you really can't live without a Dino, which is the best one to go for? In view of the foregoing it would make sense to buy one as young as possible and with the lowest possible mileage on it. Certainly it will be expensive but if it is well maintained and regularly serviced whilst in your possession then its value will steadily increase. The targa-topped GTS being harder to find is naturally going to have a higher initial price and one would expect to see its value rise accordingly. If the trends of the last few years are anything to go by then the Dino, like any other Ferrari, can be a wise and enjoyable investment. It's certainly more fun, (though not necessarily as nail-biting) than watching the stocks and shares go up and down.

The obvious places to look for a Dino are in the motoring magazines that specialise in classic and collectors cars. Here one can find the specialist dealers adverts, and quite often the private enthusist who has one for sale. One could also contact the Ferrari Owners Club, there is one in the UK and one in the USA, and also there is The Ferrari Club of America. Any of these clubs are likely to have members with Dinos for sale. To sum up, buy the best you can and look after it!

CLUBS, SPECIALISTS & BOOKS

Clubs

The Ferrari Owners Club is the only club that caters for Dino 246 owners, as they are accepted under the Ferrari umbrella. The club publishes a quarterly magazine, and a bi-monthly newsletter in which one can find cars and parts advertised for sale. The many club events, both social and sporting will give one the chance to meet fellow Dino owners. This can be most useful if one is looking for spare parts, or needs to know which Fiat parts were used on the Dino. At a recent meeting there were about twelve Dinos gathered together. The club also hires various race tracks for club members' use, thereby giving the owner a chance to use the car's full performance without drawing unneccessary attention. The UK club has also organised a series of Ferrari only races, so if you fancy yourself as the reincarnation of Nuvolari then that could be for you.

More comprehensive details can be obtained by writing to:

Mr. Godfrey Eaton
Ferrari Owners Club
10 Whittox Lane
Frome
Somerset BA11 1BY

In America the two clubs are:

Ferrari Club of America
2000 Webber Hills Rd
Wayzata
Minnesota 55391
USA

Ferrari Owners Club USA
15910 Ventura Boulevard
Suite 1201
Encino
Ca 91436
USA

Specialists

There are many good engineering workshops, and most Dino owners have their own favourites when it comes to having work done, so the following list is not exhaustive, but includes those who offer a comprehensive service.

Maranello Concessionaires
Thorpe Industrial Estate
Ten Acre Lane
Thorpe
Egham
Surrey TW20 8RJ
Official Ferrari importer for the UK with experience of all types of Ferraris.

DK Engineering
Unit D
200 Rickmansworth Rd.
Watford
Herts WD1 7JS
Restoration specialist, with numerous concours wins.

Graypaul Motors
The Coneries
Loughborough
Leics LE11 1DZ
Well known for restoration work, and very large stock of spares for out-of-production Ferraris.

Modena Engineering
Station Garage
East Horsley
Surrey
Enthusiastic dealer with good selection of second-hand Ferraris.

Dino Services
Unit 7
Endsleigh Rd Ind. Est.
Norwood Green
Heston
Middx UB2 5QN
Specialises in Dinos. All work, even re-upholstering done in house.

Nick Cartwright Specialist Cars
Cedar Lodge
Greenaway Ln
Hackney
Matlock
Derbyshire
Dino owner; restores and sells Dinos.

Denny Schue
6305 Monero Drive
Rancho Palos Verdes
California 90274
USA
If you own, or have owned a Dino then let Denny Schue know. He is trying to compile a definitive Dino register, but can only do it with your assistance. Write to Denny for details.

Books

There are now about 150 books that have the name Ferrari in the title, but as some of them cover a particular type only you'll no doubt be pleased to know that you won't need to buy them all. The following, about Ferrari generally, can be recommended.
The Complete Ferrari by Godfrey Eaton. Cadogan Books, 1986
An ideal reference book, gives brief specifications of hundreds of

different Ferraris, with many photos to aid identification.

Ferrari (6th ed.) by Tanner and Nye. Haynes, 1984.
Excellent, though expensive; 660 pages with hundreds of photos. Sixth edition has expanded section on Ferrari road cars.

Ferrari, the Sports and GT cars by Fitzgerald, Merritt and Thompson. PSL, 1979.
Doesn't cover the Grand Prix cars, but coverage of GT cars is unsurpassed. Could do with updating now.

Enzo Ferrari, 50 years of greatness by Piero Casucci. Haynes, 1982.
Puts over the character of Ferrari and the vast range of cars that have been produced bearing his name.

The following books are specifically about the Ferraris that have been labelled Dino.

Ferrari Dino 206GT, 246GT by Ian Webb. Osprey, 1980.
Well researched book about all the V-6 engined Dino road cars.

Dino, the little Ferrari by Doug Nye. Osprey, 1979.
Covers all the V6 and V8 engined Ferraris from 1957 – 1979, including the single seat F1 and F2 cars.

Ferrari Dino 1965 – 1974.
Brooklands Books, 1986
Reprints of road tests and other Dino articles from magazines like *Road & Track, Autocar* and others.

Models

The Dino has been produced in model form in all sizes, from a $^{1}/_{4}$ scale GTS pedal car down to a two inch long diecast toy, and in between someone has produced a 1:12 scale bottle and the same size lamp. The following are amongst the more than thirty kits and models of The Dino 246 that have been produced.

246GT	Aoshima 802	Plastic kit	1:20 scale
246GT	Crown 5	Plastic kit	1:24
246GT	Crown 2	Plastic kit	1:35
246GT	Shinsei 405	Metal diecast	1:38
246GT	Cam F-003	Metal hand-built	1:43
246GT	Record	Resin kit & built	1:43
246GT	Western Models 107	Metal kit & built	1:43
246GTS	Western Models 107X	Metal kit & built	1:43
246GTS	Record	Resin kit & built	1:43
246GT	Sakura 8	Metal diecast	1:43
246GTS	Modern Classics	Metal kit	1:24

246GT as reced by NART at Le Mans in 1972 has been modeled in 1:43 scale by three companies, the best, in my opinion being the resin model by Starter of France. No doubt there will be even more models of the Dino 246GT as it becomes more appreciated as a classic.

1

PHOTO GALLERY

1. The first styling exercise on a Dino 206S chassis, the 'Dino Berlinetta Speciale', has certain features that later appeared on the production Dinos. Particularly noticeable is the cockpit profile, the elongated recessed scoop just below the side windows and the wrap-around rear window. (Pininfarina)

2. This head-on shot of the 'Dino Berlinetta Speciale' highlights the headlight arrangement that Pininfarina adapted to the Fiat Dino. (Pininfarina)

3. At the Turin show in November 1966 Pininfarina displayed this 'Dino Berlinetta GT'. The 206 Dino shape is almost complete, although a number of details have still to be changed. Note, especially, the racing style windscreen wiper and the five-star wheels (Pininfarina)

4. The same car from the rear shows the one piece engine and luggage bay cover that was hinged into the roof. This was later changed to two separate covers, which is more practical. (Pininfarina)

2

3

4

5

6

7

5. A year later, in 1967, the 'Dino Coupé GT' was presented. The absence of quarter-lights distinguishes it from the production cars. (Pininfarina)

6. At the back the Dino now has the separate engine and luggage bay covers, and the twinned rear lights. (Pininfarina)

7. The profile of the Dino accentuates the subtle curves that effectively make the Dino appear smaller than it actually is. The 206GT has uncovered chrome filler cap, and knock-off wheels. (Pininfarina)

8

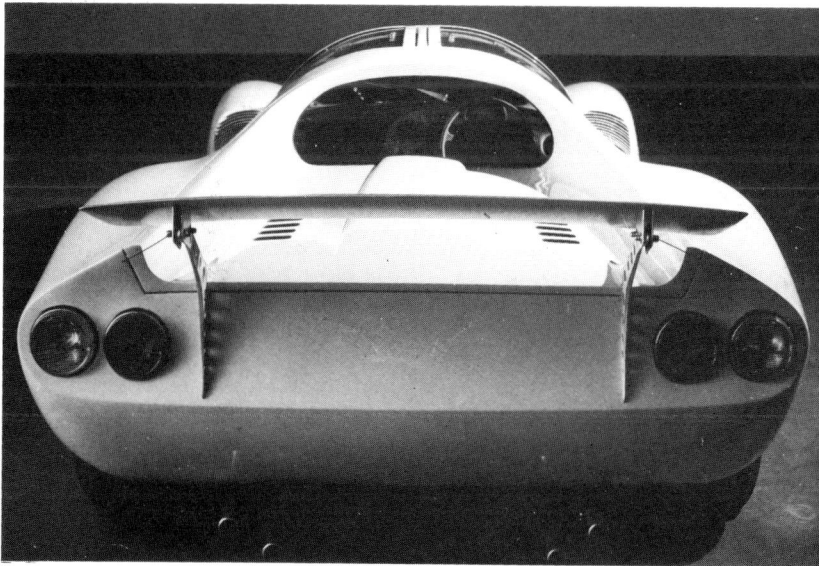

9

10

11

12

8 & 9. At Frankfurt in 1967 this unusual design on a 206S chassis was displayed. Described as a 'Berlinetta Prototipo Competizione' it never raced. Indeed one would question the desirability of an almost totally glass roof on a competition car. (Pininfarina)

10 – 12. The Dino script appears numerous times on the car. The Script is a stylised copy of Dino Ferrari's signature. Script on the tail panel has the letters GT added.

13

14

15

13. This is the 'Dino' badge to be found on the nose of the car. It is telling that the Ferrari prancing horse badge was not to be found (ex-works) on any examples of this 'almost a Ferrari'.

14. Round rear lights like these were traditional on Ferraris for many years. Chrome Prancing Horse has been added by owner.

15. Rear bumper on early cars incorporates rear number plate light. Black rubber strip is more for style than anything else.

16. Number plate light on later models is fitted to luggage bay cover. Note also single reversing lamp.

16

17

18

17 & 18. Dinos were available with or without perspex headlight covers. The covers were probably good for one extra mph on the top speed. US regulations didn't allow them at all.

19. Side scoops are functional, not just for show, allowing unimpeded air to route directly to the carburettor-mounted air filter.

20. Door handle is unobtrusive, and the same as fitted to the Ferrari Daytona.

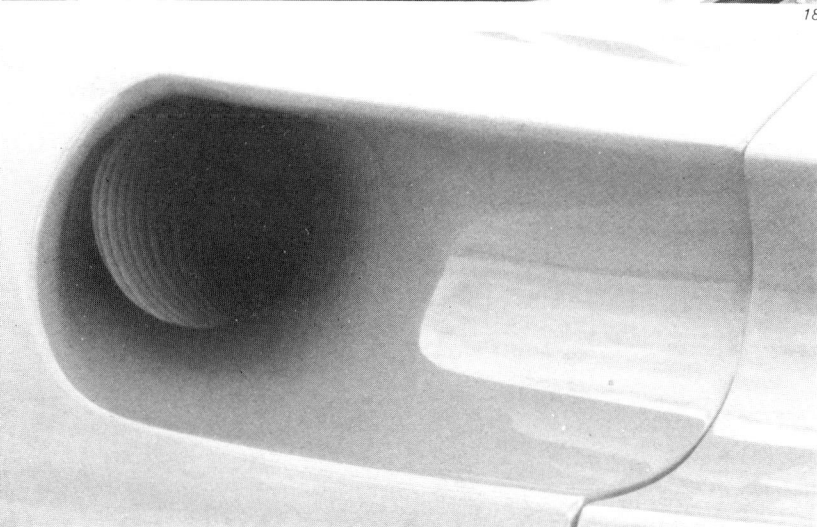

19

20

21

22

23

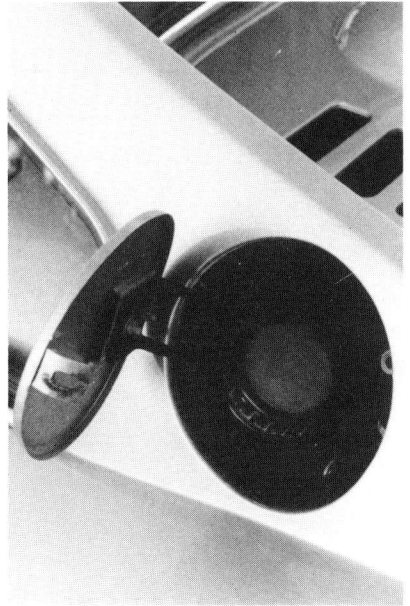

24

21. Guess who designed this one?

22. Unusual rear window design improved rear three quarter-vision considerably. Chrome trim is effective styling ploy. Slots in engine cover allow hot air to escape.

23 & 24. On 246GTs the filler cap was fitted behind a round cover that was released from inside the car.

25

26

27

25 & 26. The differences between the GT and GTS models can be seen easily in these two photos. Notice that on the GTS the rear side window is replaced by a slotted panel.

27. The GTS roof unclips from the rear, and is stowed neatly behind the seats.

28. Interior of the Dino is spacious and comfortable for two. Note the headlining of roof stowed behind the seats.

28

29. Seats have one piece shell and backs are not adjustable. Gated gear-lever is Ferrari tradition.

29

30. Dashboard is same as in the Ferrari Daytona, but main instruments are partly obscured by driver's hands. The button in dash centre resets the trip counter.

31 & 32. Different interior trims are a result of owners' personal preferences. Quarter-light catches quite often come unstuck.

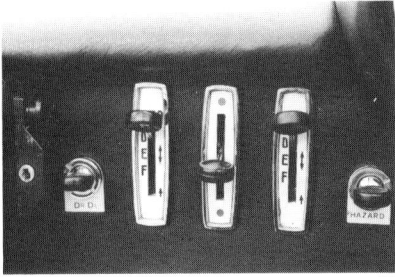

33. Centre of dash board has switches for heater controls.

34. The forward bank of cylinders is hidden under the rear bulkhead and is only accessible through detachable panels in the wheel arches, or by dropping the complete engine out.

35. Engine fills compartment and is hidden under large air filter.

34

35

36

37

38

36 & 38. 246GT looks good from all angles. This particular example has non-standard exterior mirror, and painted spokes in the wheels.

39 & 40. This GTS has the more normal silver painted wheels. Wheel arches have a small lip and body has subtle crease along flank at bumper height.

41. Ready for inspection. The various opening parts cover, from front to back, the spare wheel, the engine and the luggage compartment. Each one, including the filler cap is relased from inside car.

42. Spare wheel is a very snug fit, and not easy to lift out.

43. Spare wheel shares space with fuse boxes and brake servo assembly.

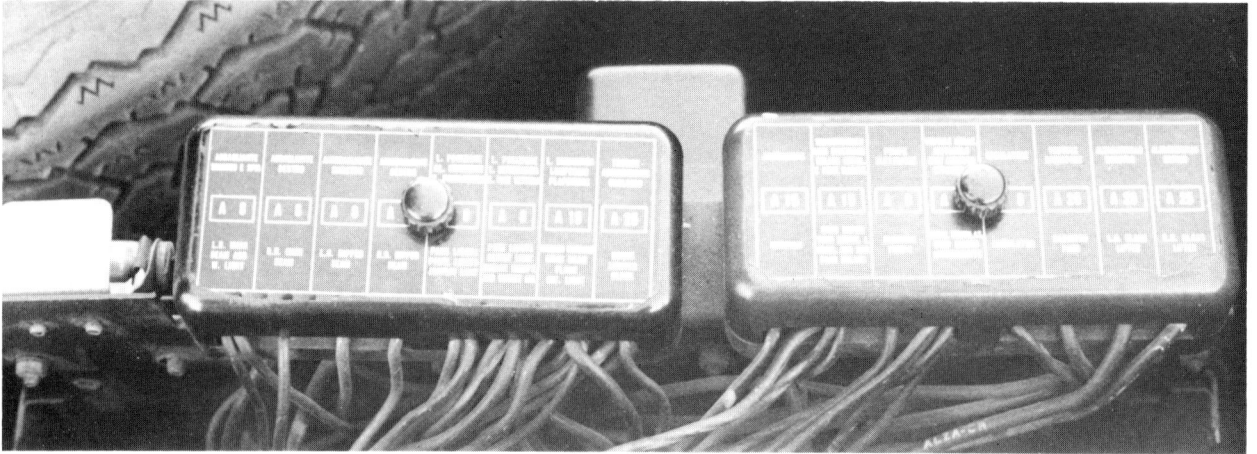
44

44. Fuses are clearly marked with size required and function.

45. Boot is a reasonable size for a sports car, and will take nearly six cubic feet of luggage in small and medium size cases, if packed carefully.

46. Also in the boot is the spare coil in case the main system fails.

47. Tool kit and jack are part of standard fittings.

45

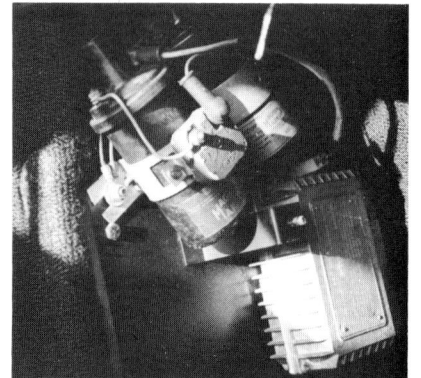
46

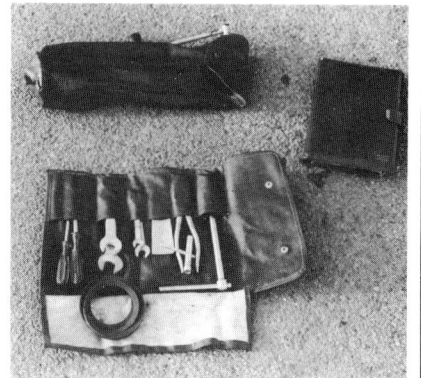
47

48

48. This is the engine of an original version showing the ex-works type of finish.

49. Front indicator on UK Dinos was flush with the bodywork. US Dinos had these lights mounted vertically which rather spoilt the line. Note the small repeater indicator on the wing.

50 & 51. Jeff Simpson races his standard Dino to great effect. With race number 10c he was part of the Ferrari team in the Oulton Park 4-hour relay in September 1985. He also regularly hill-climbs his car. (Jeff Simpson collection)

49

50

51

52. Elwynne Owen-Jones has modifed his Dino considerably for hill-climbs and racing. This Dino was a very rusty 'M' registration car before being prepared for competition (author).

53. Bumpers have been removed to save weight, and oil cooler is mounted beneath radiator opening. Brake ducts have been enlarged resulting in a more aggressive appearance (author).

54. Rear arches have been flared slightly to cover the wider Avon racing tyres. Engine compartment has been opened up internally and hot air now vents through luggage cover louvres and the large holes within the number plate (author).

55. Front screen is replaced with polycarbonate example, side windows are perspex and the doors have been reskinned in aluminium. Extinguisher and ignition cut-out switches are mounted externally for safety reasons (author).

56

56. Oil filler cap is mounted externally, and extra cooling slots are cut into lower bodywork. Wheels are non-Ferrari items (author).

57. Engine is heavily modified and has petrol injection fitted. It also has Cosworth pistons, larger valves, reground cams and dry sump arrangement. Power is estimated to be 245bhp @ 7,500rpm. There is a photo of the engine in the 'colour section' (author).

57

58. Interior trim and door panels have been removed to
save weight, and Tachometer mounted on dashboard.
Fire extinguisher system is also fitted (author).

59. Another, less radical, approach to racing. This time
with front and rear spoilers fitted (author).

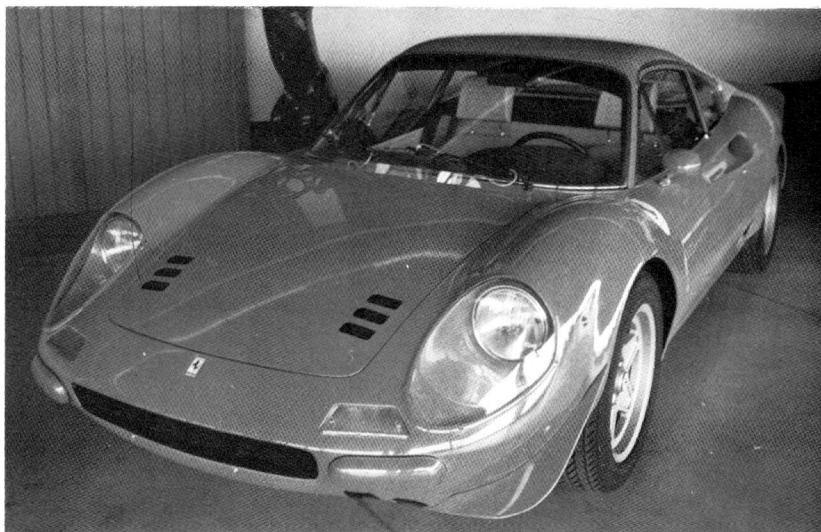